Contents

C000149337

Before you dip your toes

Lincolnshire has over 50 miles of, mostly unspoilt, coastline stretching from the Humber Estuary in the North to the Wash in the South. I know of no other coastline where almost all of it can be walked continuously along the beach (with due care and attention for incoming tides). What other county has not one, but two of Britain's historically most significant trading ports? Where else can you find seals breeding on a bomb site? The Lincolnshire Coast is full of treasures. When I wrote an earlier book about the Yorkshire Coast I spent no little time considering what constitutes a coastline, so I won't trample on old ground again but I will add that this time, with a considerably shorter stretch of coastline to work with than in Yorkshire, I have allowed my definition of "Coast" to include venues up to 10 miles from the seafront.

The word *dynamic* is often used to describe a person full of energy, and there is no doubt that it is energy that entitles the Lincolnshire Coast to be called *dynamic* in the other sense of the word – in that it is constantly changing. Much like the Holderness Coast further North, two tides a day, every day, are nibbling away at the coastline removing clay, sand, shingle and soil before depositing it further down the coast. As you will read later, sometimes these "nibbles" become more like dirty great big bites!

Don't expect this book to spoon-feed you with a list of must-visit spots, we are all different and what appeals to one is most definitely not someone else's cup of tea. I'll be very disappointed, however, if, after reading the book, you haven't made your own top-ten places to explore in the near future.

But, how should you use the book? I'm one of those odd people who likes to pick a book up and thumb through the pages from the back to the front. Should you be more conventional and follow the book from beginning to end, be prepared for a few surprises. For example, *"G is for Gibraltar – A Point to Prove"* is as you might expect, all about Gibraltar Point, whereas *"T is for Trades ..."* will take you on a historical tour around some of Boston's important industries.

Should you prefer to read about specific places all in one go, my advice is to use the *Quick A to Z Location Guide*.

It is possible that your particular favourite spot might not appear in this book – in 55,000 words I just cannot cover everywhere. Rather than leaving disappointed, I hope that you will take the opportunity to find out about a few new places or maybe take the chance to reacquaint yourself with a couple of long-lost friends.

On the subject of photographs, the lack of them is down to a simple factor – memory. No, it wasn't that I forgot to put any in, it's simply the case that every photograph adds to the file size, which in turn increases the price that you must pay for the book. If you want to look through tens of thousands of Lincolnshire Coast photos without spending a penny, then go no further than Wikimedia and its search box at:

https://commons.wikimedia.org/wiki/Main_Page?uselang=en-gb

A brief but important word on accessibility. Some places are reached on roads, others on footpaths, disused railway lines, beaches etc. Additionally, some of the venues are in the hands of private owners who will have their own views on accessibility. Furthermore, locations change, often overnight. A clear, flat sandy beach one day can be rough and rocky the next. A wide level clifftop path can overnight be lost completely following a landslip leading to a different (and possibly completely unsuitable) route being necessary. Therefore, I have chosen to make no claims regarding suitability for wheelchair and other disabled users. I hope you will understand why. That said, I can recommend a look at the wildlife trust/nature reserve websites. Both organisations take accessibility very seriously and publish an assortment of accessible paths, trails and other services online.

Finally, I hope you will make good use of the "Further Reading" possibilities. Every book recommendation is taken from my personal collection, amassed at surprisingly little expense. Should you wish to purchase any of them, do shop around – not one of them cost me more than a fiver – including postage! Almost all the older books are out of copyright and have been digitised on websites such as archive.org and Google books. Consequently, there is a real goldmine of free-to-read material. Regarding the online content, please remember that websites change over time and so although each one has been checked (and virus scanned), I cannot accept any responsibility for content, safety etc.

Now that's out of the way, it's time to pull off the socks, roll up the trousers and get those feet well and truly wet as we explore the Lincolnshire Coast - from A to Z.

Quick A – Z Location Guide

Each location is followed by capital letters pointing you at the relevant chapters:

Alford.................................A, M, O, Q, S, U

Anderby Creek...............................M, O, S, V

Barrow-upon-Humber.................M, Z

Boston.................................A, F, I, M, P, R, T, U, V, W, X, Z

Chapel St. Leonards......................E, O, U, W, Y

Cleethorpes.................................A, B, E, H, I, K, N, P, Q, V, W, Y, Z

Freiston Shore..............................B, Z

Friskney...F, G, R, U

Gibraltar Point................................B, E, F, G, H, R

Grimsby...A, C, D, E, I, K, L, M, N, P, V, X, Y, Z

Holbeach.................................A, R, U, Z

Humberston.................................A, E, H, U

Huttoft...O, V

Immingham.................................A, C, Z

Ingoldmells.................................E, H, O, R, W

Killingholme.................................A, C

Mablethorpe.................................A, B, C, E, M, N, Q, S, U, V, W, Y

Saltfleet/Saltfleetby......................B, M, S, V

Sandilands.................................H, O

Skegness.................................A, B, D, E, H, I, O, Q, R, S, T, U, W, Y

A is for 'Orses and an Anglo-American Agreement

I'm too young to have seen or heard the comedy double act of Clapham and Dwyer who were at their peak of popularity when my Dad was growing up. However, his regular renditions of an adapted version of a 1930's recording of their *Cockney Alphabet* was a memorable feature of my childhood.

Dad's version began something like this ...

A is for 'Orses (Hay is for Horses)

B for Dinner (Beef for Dinner

C for th'ighlanders (Seaforth Highlanders Regiment)

D for 'Ential (Deferential)

E for Adam (Eve or Adam)

F for 'vescence (Effervescence)

And so it went on.

Clapham and Dwyer made regular music hall appearances all over the country, including several venues near to the Lincolnshire coastline. Concert Halls in Louth, Grimsby, Cleethorpes and Skegness can all claim to have hosted the popular radio entertainers.

But it is A for 'orses that we will start our alphabetical tour with – a guide to agriculture in Lincolnshire, particularly in the vicinity of the coast, and a look at some of the surprising ways horses have been used in the area, before telling how the Pilgrim Fathers came to be associated with South Lincolnshire.

Agriculture might not sound like the most exciting topic to many readers, but to tell the story of farming in the region requires examination of Lincolnshire's coastal geography, and particularly significant recent changes to the area.

From Skegness southwards coastal land is entirely alluvial drift and boulder clay with a little peat thrown in for good measure. As a result, this area – part of the Fens that stretches over five counties, is very marshy, supports a varied and rich habitat and requires a very different approach to farming.

Fenland is predominately within a few feet of sea level and has historically been prone to severe flooding. Left uncultivated, fresh and saltwater marshland dominates. However, much of the land has been artificially drained and then enclosed by high embankments and given further protection from flood waters by installing pumps and drainage ditches. The result is some of the best quality arable and vegetable farming land in England. So much of it that the Fens of South Lincolnshire, Cambridgeshire, Norfolk, Suffolk and Huntingdonshire contain more than half of all the Grade I agricultural land in England.

Between Skegness and Humberston, the mix of boulder clay and alluvial drift continues but becomes a much narrower "*spit*" of between 1 and 4 miles across before giving way to a wide expanse of chalk and Lower Greensand. Like the Fens, this is a naturally fertile area – Greensand is an excellent natural source of potassium, ideal for organic farming.

From Humberston, moving North and Westwards into the Humber Estuary, much of the coastal land is developed in the form of Cleethorpes and Grimsby. After that, Immingham, Killingholme (North and South) and East Halton are largely taken up with massive chemical plants before farmland begins to take over once again.

Agricultural statistics for the coastal regions are not compiled to the best of my knowledge, but I am aware of DEFRA calculations in 2006 revealing the county of Lincolnshire to be responsible for almost a quarter of the UK's horticultural output, and, of that, almost two fifths of all bulbs and flowers are grown in the county. One in eight of all the potatoes grown in the United Kingdom come from farms in Lincolnshire. More than 10% of the total wheat and oilseed rape crops can be traced back to Lincolnshire farmers. Vitally for the people of the county, Agriculture is responsible for employing one in ten of the population. Bearing in mind that Lincolnshire has less than 5% of all the UK's farmland, these figures are all the more remarkable.

The most southerly part of the Lincolnshire coastline is in the district of South Holland. The name *"Holland"* originates in the Netherlands, where North and South Holland are two large coastal regions within the nation of The Netherlands. Although the names Holland and Netherlands are commonly interchanged outside of the country itself, be careful if visiting The Netherlands as many there are offended by visitors referring to the whole country by using the part-name of two of its coastal territories. That was the easy part. Now to clear up what the word Holland actually means. Throughout Lincolnshire you will likely come across people who will tell you it is derived from hollow-land due to the low-lying nature of much of the county and the country on the other side of the North Sea. Not so, I'm afraid. Even the otherwise outstanding book *Wide Horizons*, written in and about South Holland gets it wrong – claiming that Holland comes from High Land since much of the reclaimed land is higher than the surrounding fens and the sea. I found no evidence to support this theory. What is clear, from several sources, is that the name Holland emerged from a middle Dutch term *holtland*, with a holt being a wooded area. You don't need to spend long looking at an aerial view of the Dutch coastline to find large expanses of forest; to the west of Bergen and Haarlem for example. So, South Holland, almost entirely agricultural land dotted with villages and towns must simply take its name from its cousin across the sea.

Since this is a book about the coast, whilst considering South Holland, perhaps it is worth taking a look at how it has changed in recent history. The book *Wide Horizons* (a free download, by the way) includes a helpful map suggesting that Holbeach, Spalding, Surfleet and Gosberton would all have been on the coast in Roman times. Places such as Guy's Head, Dawsmere, even the inappropriately named Seas End were all well and truly under water at that time. So, what happened?

But we do not have the Romans to thank for the development of South Holland as an agricultural (and, subsequently, horticultural) hotbed. Rather, it was the opportunism of local Britons who could see the coastline gradually receding, exposing fertile silt beds and an environment ripe for extracting salt from the saline coastal waters. As time marched on during the first four centuries after Christ, more and more of the newly available land was used for arable and pastoral farming. A combination of these uses of the land along with the contraction of peat beds created firm raised banks known locally as *roddons* – ideal for establishing settlements above the soil that still flooded from time to time. And so, the area grew and grew, geographically and commercially. So much so, that some estimate as much as 30-40 square miles of "new" land has been formed, and subsequently farmed in the last two millennia.

Farming Salt was, and still is, a year round job – not seasonal, in other words. Evidence of salt production going back two thousand years and more has been found in several places including Pinchbeck, Holbeach St Johns, Cowbit and Spalding. Nowadays salt is a household product routinely added as a flavouring to most savoury (and some sweet) dishes but for millennia it has been invaluable as a preservative for fish and meat.

In contrast to South Holland, New Holland is at the opposite end of the Lincolnshire coast. If you've read my companion volume about the Yorkshire coast, you'll recall the difficulties involved in determining where a coastline ends and a riverbank starts. No such difficulties on this occasion. The positioning and naming of the port of New Holland almost directly on the opposite side of the Humber to Hull gave me an easy option. Lincolnshire coastline for me, therefore runs from New Holland in the North to South Holland and the border with Norfolk.

To the west of New Holland, the land rises gradually to meet what are known as the Lincolnshire Wolds. There the land is mainly cretaceous chalk with a mix of alluvial deposits and (further west) rich clay, ideal for brick manufacturing. From New Holland eastwards and south there were once several pig and sheep farms interspersed between fields of arable crops. The pier and railway station at New Holland were intended to connect North Lincolnshire and the south with Hull and all points north. For a while after the station opened in 1848, the signs were good. Passenger and freight numbers exceeded hopes, but it was not to last. Requiring goods and people to combine rail transport with a ferry crossing was both inconvenient and time consuming. When Hull became directly connected to Doncaster by Rail, farmers and passengers soon discovered that more mileage did not mean a longer journey in terms of time. Between the two world wars, pier traffic was probably at its peak. At this time, the pier was handling well over 1000 head of livestock every day and up to 30 times that number of paying passengers. The figures for cattle and sheep help to illustrate the trend nowadays towards arable and vegetable farming. Very few dairy, pig or sheep farms remain in this area. The pier still operates, but the railway station closed on the same day in 1981 that the Humber Bridge opened to traffic.

So, we have seen that the Lincolnshire coast is very varied in terms of agricultural possibilities and how the people of Lincolnshire have shown great courage and determination to make the most of what they have beneath their feet, even when standing knee-deep in mud and water. This is a good point to move on to look at some more people of faith, fortitude and no shortage of bravery – the people who became known as the Pilgrim Fathers.

During the reign of Elizabeth I, Protestantism was returning to the ascendancy, but it was a time of turmoil. Elizabeth's route to the throne needs to be told in order to understand the religious climate of the period a little better. So we will leave the Lincolnshire coast briefly to consider this matter.

Henry VIII, Elizabeth's father, a Catholic, had instigated what became known as the English Reformation, by which the Church of England broke away from the Roman Catholic Church and direct Papal rule. Motivated more by political and personal necessity than theology he also brought in the *Divine Right of Kings*, effectively making himself second in authority only to God and therefore immune from earthly prosecution. This had also allowed him to accuse, charge, and often execute, any of his opponents as heretics at will.

On his death, Henry was succeeded by his nine-year-old son Edward, who steered (some might say crashed) his kingdom into full-on Protestantism for the first time. Of course, being only a child, responsibility must rest with his most senior advisers, particularly the Archbishop of Canterbury, Thomas Cranmer. The poor lad never made it to adulthood, passing away three months shy of his sixteenth birthday. Fearing a return to Catholicism, the young King and his council nominated his first cousin Lady Jane Grey as his successor to the crown, effectively snubbing both of his half sisters, Mary and Elizabeth.

Edward died on 6th July 1553 and four days later Lady Jane Grey reluctantly accepted the title of Queen. Before a coronation could be organised, Mary, a Catholic remember, had rounded up sufficient support for the Privy Council to declare her Queen instead. By the 19th July, Mary was in London as monarch in waiting and Lady Jane Grey was imprisoned along with her husband.

Both were beheaded seven months later. The *nine-day Queen* as some have called her, thus became the second teenage monarch to die within a year. The new Queen, Mary, also earned a nickname – *Bloody Mary*. Her restoration of Catholicism brought with it a five-year period of intense persecution for the nation's protestants. Almost three hundred were burned alive for their apparent dissent. Even the dead bodies of several others with similar religious convictions were exhumed and burned as heretics.

In Lincolnshire, although no protestants were burned at the stake in Mary's reign, many from the neighbouring counties of Yorkshire, Derbyshire and Norfolk had been. Also during Henry VIII's final year of rule, Anne Askew, of Stallingborough, near Grimsby on the North Lincolnshire coast, found herself imprisoned and tortured. Her father, William, a cruel and wealthy landowner and member of the King's court had forced Anne to marry Thomas Kyme, a Catholic farmer and landowner from Friskney near Wainfleet. It was a brutal marriage and, in spite of two children together, Anne left her husband and moved to London. Anne's subsequent autobiographical *Examinations* chronicled her life, faith and persecution and is considered an essential and unique account of sixteenth century Protestant life under extreme Catholic duress. Anne refused to renounce her faith or to disclose the names of other protestants – even under torture. When taken to be burned, along with other prisoners, Anne was offered a final opportunity to be pardoned. Anne apparently listened attentively to the Bishop of Salisbury, Nicholas Shaxton as he delivered a final sermon. The Bishop had met Anne before and been told by her that it would have been better for him that he had never been born, so he was probably not surprised when she punctuated his sermon repeatedly with the same phrase *"there he misseth, and speaketh without the book"*.

Queen Mary died in November 1558 and was succeeded by her Protestant younger half-sister Elizabeth in spite of Mary's failed attempts to produce an heir or to get Elizabeth to marry a Catholic. Elizabeth, or *Good Queen Bess* as she became popularly known, was more moderate and mild in manner than her predecessors. She sought wise counsel and quickly re-established the Protestant Church with herself as Supreme Governor. However, this did not signal an end to religious persecution. Even Elizabeth herself continued with executions of people considered to be protestant extremists.

Elizabeth's attempts to unify people under what would later become known as the Church of England only served to antagonise further many groups of protestant worshippers. Her *Act of Uniformity* passed into law in 1559 and made it a legal requirement for all to attend church once a week or face a fine of a shilling. The new law also forced churches to use the *book of common prayer* in all services.

In Gainsborough, under the leadership of John Smyth, one group of what many would now call *Separatists* are now acknowledged to be a founding group of the Baptist Church. Over the county border, in Scrooby, Nottinghamshire, another congregation under the ministry of Richard Clyfton was rapidly expanding. Clyfton was a Brownist, following the teachings of the Separatist, Robert Browne. (In fact for over 200 years, what we now call the Pilgrims were known as the Brownists). When King James VI of Scotland took to the English throne in 1603 his attempts to unify the nations extended to religion in many ways. Firstly, he offered a conditional olive branch of sorts to the many Catholics under his rule. All had to sign an oath of allegiance in return for a promise not to persecute *"any that will be quiet and give but an outward obedience to the law"*. As for the many groups of Separatists, hopes were high at first, but the Hampton Court Conference of 1604 gave them just one of the concessions they were asking for – a unified English Bible for the first time (The King James Version). Aside from that, all they got was further persecution. In the following year Richard Clyfton was declared a non-conformist and removed from his position. Others were given heavy fines and/or imprisonment.

Little wonder then, that Separatist groups began to collaborate and form a view that their time in England was up. In 1607 a large group from the Scrooby area decided to join with a smaller group from Gainsborough and set up new lives in the more liberal Holland across the North Sea, even though such a journey would be illegal – travelling without a permit could lead to long spells in prison, if caught. The Gainsborough group were successful in reaching Leiden but the Scrooby Separatists suffered a terrible betrayal. Their story was preserved by William Bradford, a native of Austerfield, just over the county border in Yorkshire, in his account of the early years of the Pilgrim Fathers – *Of Plymouth Plantation*.

Bradford related the tale of a large group (exact number not known, but of the order of 20 men, women and children) who gathered in the Lincolnshire port of Boston where the company *"hired a ship wholly to themselves and made agreement with the master to be ready at a certain day, and take them and their goods in at a convenient place, where they accordingly would all attend in readiness"*. Why Boston? At the time, Boston was second only to London in terms of its size as a port. In spite of rapid silting, which is why modern-day Boston is now considered to be over three miles from the open sea, Boston attracted vast amounts of shipping and so was considered the port most likely to attract a captain willing to be paid to carry a large number of law-breakers.

After several days in waiting, the ship's master came one night and prepared them to for the voyage. They had not gone far when they were betrayed. At Scotia Creek, a few miles downriver from Boston the master *"put them into open boats, and there rifled and ransacked them, searching to their shirts for money, yea even the women further than became modesty; and then carried them back into the town and made them a spectacle and wonder to the multitude which came flocking on all sides to behold them"*. In 1957, a granite memorial was erected close to the spot of the betrayal, 350 years after the arrest of the Scrooby Separatists. It is located within the Havenside Country Park and Nature Reserve, facing the river on the North bank of the Haven.

In Boston, the Pilgrims were subjected to further ransacking leaving them without money and other possessions including their precious literature. Most were imprisoned for a month in the Guildhall (seven received longer sentences) before being sent back to their homes in Nottinghamshire. Visitors to the Guildhall, which has stood since 1390 can tour an authentic courtroom and the prison cells where some of the Pilgrim Fathers were held as well as seeing a permanent exhibition dedicated to Boston's Pilgrim Fathers.

The following year, along with others, most of the Scrooby Separatists tried again – this time successfully, but made their escape from Hull, not Boston. However, Boston was far from done with its association with the Pilgrim Fathers. Curiously, just a handful of years after the town had jailed people for their puritanical beliefs it appointed a Puritan, John Cotton, as minister of St. Botolph's Church. Cotton's approach was a gentle one – he sought to reform the Church of England from within. As a result, his ministry thrived. His church, The Boston Stump, was already a significant landmark with its distinctive 270-foot tower being visible as far away as Norfolk on the other side of the Wash. His consensual preaching style attracted more and more parishioners until the Anglican church once again began to exert more pressure on its priests to conform.

Cotton was forced into hiding at first, but having decided the situation was not likely to improve in his lifetime, he and his wife followed other pilgrims across the Atlantic to America and Massachusetts. Arriving there in 1633 Cotton settled in what had recently been named Boston having previously been known as *Trimountaine* in recognition of three hills which have long since been lost as the city developed. As many as 1 in 10 of Boston's seventeenth century population are believed to have ended up in their American namesake.

Boston in Lincolnshire is officially twinned with the French town of Laval, but Boston, Lincs. and Boston, Ma. have maintained a close friendship. The *"Historic Bostons Partnership"* celebrates the connection between the two Bostons. Every year on 7th September, Charter Day commemorates the renaming of the Massachusetts city in 1630.

In The Stump, two stained glass windows commemorate the Pilgrims. One shows John Cotton saying farewell to his congregation as he and his wife prepare to board their ship for America. The second is dedicated to Anne Bradstreet, the daughter of Thomas Dudley, steward of the Earl of Lincoln. Her Husband, Simon, of the Lincolnshire Fen village of Horbling, was a

16

founder of the city of Boston. Anne is considered an important figure in American literature since she was the first female American writer to have work published and, although she was a Puritan herself, through her writings she frequently challenged the established view that a woman's place was in the home carrying out domestic chores, and, thus became revered as an early campaigner for women's rights.

Before we move on, I have one more story to tell – again of a migration of sorts. This time, though, the people involved didn't leave the country, or even the county in most instances. And they returned home again after a few days. If they were lucky, they got to do it every year. The annual event happened on the 14th May and went by the name of *Pag Rag Day*.

Pag Rag Day signalled the start (and end for many) of the one and only holiday of the year for most people employed in service. It also served as a time for recruitment. Thousands of servants, maids, cooks, gardeners and housekeepers got a single day's paid holiday every year prior to the 1871 Bank Holidays Act. Many took May 14th as a day to take an excursion to the coast, while others used the day off to attend one of the many recruitment fairs taking place in market squares throughout the country. Why the name *"Pag Rag"* you might ask? The traditional view is that service staff went out on this day with laundry packed in a bag – packed rags perhaps? In Latin, the verb *pagare* means to pay, so it possibly has a European origin as a pay day. However, the *Lincolnshire Echo* offered an alternative view in 1935:

> *"Tuesday was pag rag day in the country, farm servants who are not confined workers and who have not been retained for another year then preparing for their move. Pag-rag day is sometimes thought to mean pack-rag" day. but I am told that " in this case actually means carry." the phrase signifying removal. Farm servants come into (Lincoln), where they stand along the pavement edges, and farmers who want men select those whom they think suitable. If they hand the worker a "fastenpenny" (usually a shilling) the man is engaged for the year, but if he does not receive this he can, if wishes, take any other Job which Is offered to him before he goes to his new place of employment."*

The newspaper went on to explain why the tradition was fast dying out:

"The casual employment of men, as opposed to annual contract, and the use of newspaper advertisements for the exchange of employment, have made the May Hirings largely obsolete."

A report in *The Lincolnshire Chronicle* from May 1883 highlighted the earlier popularity of Pag Rag Day with service staff, grateful for their day off:

"Whit Tuesday is the regular date of Alford summer fair. This year the holiday was rendered doubly attractive by the fact that pag-rag" day, or May-day market, the servants' annual holiday, fell together. The weather was fine, and our country cousins literally came into the town by droves. An early train brought 380 and the eleven train brought 300."

This is A "for 'orses" remember, so here are a few examples of the use of horses for a range of coastal services.

As *life-savers*: the courage and selflessness of our lifeboat crews is well-documented. In November 1884, the *Lincolnshire Chronicle* brought to the attention of its readers a tragic account involving the loss of four lives – three of them equine. Responding to distress signals from a fishing vessel - the *Ransom*, the Donna Nook lifeboat crew attempted to launch their boat. A team of six horses pulled the lifeboat to the water which *"owing to the rough state of the sea ... literally rolled mountains high"*. The boat was ultimately launched but not before *"breakers completely covered the horses (throwing) the pin horse onto the truck, breaking one of the shafts."* That horse drowned, along with two others and a volunteer coastguard. For over a hundred years, coastguards used teams of horses to pull lifeboats in and out of the sea – often at great risk to the lives of the horses.

As *providers of public transport*: In the early days of Cleethorpes as a seaside resort, most day-trippers from nearby Grimsby would either walk the two-mile Grimsby Road, or take a horse and cart. This changed in 1881 with the opening of the Great Grimsby Street Tramway service in 1881. A pair of horses pulled a tramcar designed to carry 30 passengers between the centre of Grimsby and Park Street on the Grimsby-Cleethorpes boundary (adjacent to the football ground). The service was so popular, even though it did not go all the way into Cleethorpes, that the trams often seen carrying twice as many passengers as they were intended. In 1898, the line was extended to Cleethorpes seafront and a third horse added to pull the weighty trams up the sloping road approach to Cleethorpes. The response was phenomenal – for the first time the service carried over a million passengers in twelve months. By 1902, this had more than doubled. It was an important but short-lived service. Electrification of the route began at the start of the twentieth century, and by the end of World War I, the last of the horse-drawn tramcars had been taken permanently out of service. One of them found its way to Laceby Hospital where it became a play feature for children recuperating from tuberculosis. Another was bought privately and moved to the Humberston Fitties – we will read more about this place later. In Skegness, a short-lived project was the beach tramway service – the prospect of laying, and, more importantly, maintaining rail tracks on a sandy beach did not deter developers Rowley and Storr, from establishing a *"penny all the way"* service to the sea. The same nickname was also used for passengers wanting similar carriage along the promenade.

As leaders of "ducks" to water and water to "ducks": The "ducks" are of course people. In Victorian and Edwardian England, modesty dictated that bathers should enter and leave the sea without exposing themselves to the gaze of others. This was achieved by hiring a personal horse-drawn bathing machine for the day. The prospective bather(s) would enter the wheeled, wooden caravan, change into their swimwear (which was often little less than their daywear) and a horse would then pull the caravan to the sea, from where the bather(s) could descend via steps directly into the water. For some, the coldness of the sea water was off-putting, but Turkish Baths *"sprang up"* in many seaside venues, including at Skegness. In 1881 the *Lincolnshire Chronicle* announced the formation of The Skegness Turkish Hot and Cold Swimming Baths Company Limited. Premises were acquired on Scarborough Avenue, some distance from the sea – but, crucially at a low level. In other locations, such as Scarborough itself and Filey in Yorkshire, raising water from the sea was such a challenge that teams of horse-drawn carriages were employed to carry large copper tanks full of fresh salt water every day. In Skegness, pipework was laid, pumping sea water directly to the baths. The Skegness project was short-lived, with the Turkish Baths company being liquidated after just ten years, but the baths themselves remained in situ until the 1950's. Some of the pipework is still visible at low tide near the end of the pier.

We will see later how the development of tourism on the coast resulted in the movement of many thousands from rural inland Lincolnshire to the rapidly expanding resorts of Cleethorpes, Skegness and Mablethorpe, But, for now, if our geological, theological, historical and horticultural expedition through the letter A has left you a little wearisome, I suggest we take a more relaxed look at the Lincolnshire Coasts many glorious stretches of sand next, starting with a place where it was the horses themselves that were the main draw.

Further Reading:

H. H. Swinnerton & P. E. Kent, The Geology of Lincolnshire, Lincolnshire Naturalists Union (1976)

J. Keith Cheetham, On the Trail of the Pilgrim Fathers, Luath Press (2001)

B is for Big Broad Beaches

When asked to think of beaches in Lincolnshire, you'd be forgiven if the wide expanse of sand at Cleethorpes, the long golden beach at Mablethorpe or the view from the promenade at Skegness comes onto mind before any thought of Freiston Shore.

These days it is hard to believe that Freiston Shore was one of the earliest places on the Lincolnshire Coast to develop as a seaside resort or that much of its popularity stemmed from horse racing festivals which took place on the beach regularly during the nineteenth century.

Freiston Shore had two hotels, The Anchor and The Coach House. The former changed its name to the Marine Hotel in 1856, with the latter becoming The Plummers Hotel. Both helped to draw large numbers from Boston and further afield, especially for the four horse racing festivals held during the summer months each year. Between them, the two hotels could stable 48 horses and could adequately cater for the large numbers of visitors requiring accommodation for their coaches. Evening dances in each of the hotel ballrooms proved to be very popular too.

Looking at Freiston Shore now it is difficult to imagine horses galloping on the sands and bathing machines being pulled out carrying many *"desirous of enjoying the salubrious exercise of sea bathing. for which here is ample accommodation"* as William White put it in his 1842 trade directory. So what happened? Partly, the area itself has changed. A combination of the effects of accretion and flooding has turned the shore into a saltmarsh and wetland, leaving the village of Freiston itself more than half a mile further from the sea than it was a century ago. Secondly, the advent of rail travel during the middle of the nineteenth century led to the likes of Cleethorpes, Mablethorpe and Skegness developing as seaside resorts, taking away much of the trade that Freiston Shore had built up.

The concept of sea bathing as a recreation (and, as was frequently advertised – a tonic) was a relatively new one in the first half of the eighteenth century. All too often, excited visitors to the coast would hire a bathing machine and enter the water without giving much thought to personal safety – with tragic consequences. Freiston Shore did not avoid such an event. As with much of the East coast, at Freiston Shore the beach is very flat, so that sea levels can be very shallow for a considerable distance. But, at a place known locally as "the lows", there is a sudden drop – the equivalent of stepping off a cliff into deep water. In August 1846 one group of men from Stamford had arrived early for the horse races, and, with time to spare, the four men hired a bathing machine.

The tide was out so the lad driving the bathing machine took the Stamford Bathers as far as he dare across the sands towards the sea at Clayhole – a distance of up to a mile and a half. Before leaving, the lad cautioned the men not to wander too far out as the water could become suddenly very deep. What happened next became national news. The *Boston Herald* reported events a few days later:

> *"for about an hour [the men] remained in the shallow water, gradually wandering towards the channel ... they came ... suddenly into upwards of 20 feet of water. The first notice they had of the fatal result which was destined to ensue from their rashness was an exclamation from Mr. Chambers to the effect that Smith was drowning and our informant (Mr. Spriggs), on looking towards the spot perceived only Mr. Smith's feet, as he sunk to rise no more. His terror now assumed a different direction, on hearing Chambers calling out for help on his own account, he felt himself to be sinking. Mr. Spriggs hastened towards him, as did also Mr. Jones, and attempted save him, but in vain, for after the former had been twice nearly involved in destruction in consequence of the desperate hold of the drowning man, they were obliged reluctantly to abandon him to his fate, and after a few struggles, Chambers also sank."*

Thomas Smith and John Chambers both lost their lives that day, a hundred and seventy years ago. Although the practice of using bathing machines has long since passed, the sea is no less dangerous than it was in those days.

A trip to Freiston Shore these days may lead to wet feet, but if you stick to the signposted paths and trails, you should not come into any further trouble than that. Much of the area is now in the care of the RSPB where the salt water lagoon offers excellent views of wading birds, often numbering up to several thousand, and the saltmarsh is a productive hunting ground for many different birds of prey. Be aware that most wading birds following migratory lifestyles, so the best advice I can offer is to check the RSPB website for up to date sightings before travelling.

As for Lincolnshire's better known beaches – at Cleethorpes, Skegness and Mablethorpe – which developed first as a seaside resort?

Perhaps a look at population figures might provide a clue. At the time of the 2001 census the population of Cleethorpes was 39,606 compared with just 284 in 1801. Mablethorpe in comparison grew from 164 to 11,780 in the same period while the population of Skegness rose from 134 to 18,910 over the equivalent two hundred years. It is worth noting at this point that the population of England was 7 times bigger after that 200-year interval, compared with Cleethorpes and Skegness being 140 times bigger while the population of Mablethorpe increased over 70-fold.

Freiston with Freiston shore (only combined figures are available) was bigger than Lincolnshire's three resort "giants" put together back in 1801. The rapid development of rail travel in the second half of the nineteenth century brought with it affordable transport for the working classes at a time when only the most wealthy had customarily made trips to the seaside. Cleethorpes was the first to be connected by railway in 1863, Skegness followed suit in 1873 with a line to Mablethorpe coming into operation in 1877. Freiston never got a railway line. Visitor numbers were already declining when a new cut in the Witham river altered the dynamics of the shoreline converting much of the sandy beach to saltmarsh in the course of a few years.

Entrepreneurs moved into the three "new" resorts, built rows of affordable homes, lodging houses and hotels, almost instantly creating jobs and places to live for thousands of working class families living in challenging urban conditions and ready for new lives by the sea. Within a generation of the railways arriving, the resident populations of Skegness, Cleethorpes and Mablethorpe had increased by 600%, 400% and 250% respectively.

In terms of beaches, just what was it that these three coastal locations could offer holidaymakers?

Cleethorpes was already known for its oysters. Fetching a price of 20 shillings for a tub of around 1000 oysters and in abundant supply, little wonder that oyster stalls along the beach proved to be a big success with visitors. The oyster beds themselves ran close to the shoreline and were seen by many curious strollers at low tide. The rapid expansion of Cleethorpes and nearby Grimsby put paid to one of its best commercial ventures though. Grimsby was becoming the biggest port in the world at that time and with the expansion came a sudden and very rapid increase in water pollution – the oyster beds were devastated.

The beach at Cleethorpes is amongst the widest in the United Kingdom. The tide goes out so far it is possible on occasions to spend most of the day on the beach without getting a good view of the sea. The length of the beach is probably most fairly measured against the lengths of the two promenades stretching out either side of the pier, and extending along Kingsway south to the leisure complex. In total, then the beach is a little over a mile and a quarter in length. When the railways first brought people to Cleethorpes the beach view was very different. The best way to describe it using a present-day landmark is to use Ross Castle. This stands at the highest point of the old clay cliff which was being rapidly eroded away. Some believe the waves caused by an increase in shipping using Grimsby had contributed to the higher erosion rate in the 1860's and 1870's. The Manchester, Sheffield & Lincolnshire Railway Company had a major investment in the town and were not going to see it literally washed away from under their feet so 17 acres of land were purchased in order to construct sea defences and landscape a promenade, incorporating as much of the old cliff as possible in the final design. The "castle" was built and named after Edward Ross, secretary of the railway company and a driving force behind the development.

Measuring the beach at Mablethorpe requires a decision to be made about the limits of the town itself. You see, Mablethorpe sits on a stretch of straight sandy coastline that is so long, it is possible to walk along the beach all the way to Skegness. So I have measured Mablethorpe's beach from the Seal Sanctuary at the Northern end of the town through to Trusthorpe Onsough Drain which bisects Mablethorpe and Trusthorpe at the Southern end. Using these terminal points Mablethorpe has a beach of just under two and a quarter glorious golden sandy miles in length. With a long promenade in front of the town itself and a wide expanse of dunes screening the beach from thousands of caravans to the north, this is one of the most attractive (and cleanest) beaches to be seen anywhere.

Evidence exists to show that Mablethorpe was expanding as a holiday destination before the railways brought a new influx of travellers. Five years before the railway line opened, William White recorded in his 1872 *"directory of Lincolnshire"* that Mablethorpe was a *"rapidly improving bathing place and village"* with *"good inns and numerous private lodging and boarding houses … much frequented during the season by visitors"*. White informed readers of a recent development – the opening of the Lincolnshire Sea Side Convalescent Home – intended to give to the working classes *"some important sanitary advantages that would otherwise be beyond their reach"*. The building, based on a design by Florence Nightingale, could accommodate 50 or so residents at a time in a building offering commanding views of the sea and with hot or cold salt water baths "on tap". Residents could stay between the months of April and November at a cost of 4 shillings per week. Unfortunately, the building was demolished in the 1980's – only photographs and pictures remain.

A glance through the pages of White's directory helps to establish the scale of Mablethorpe's emergence as a holiday resort prior to the introduction of a dedicated rail service. Alongside more than a dozen lodging houses we find the names of William Gray and Thomas Haith, both supplementing their incomes accommodating visitors by hiring out bathing machines on the seafront. But trade directories don't always tell the whole story. Gray and Haith were neighbours and just a year before William White compiled his directory, the former was recorded as a farmer in the 1871 census with the latter described merely as an agricultural labourer. Ten years later had they continued their interest in tourism? It would appear not. Gray is once again listed as a farmer, with Haith apparently now a fisherman. These and other records reveal not only the rapid growth of seaside resorts such as Mablethorpe, but also how much the resident population were prepared to adapt to meet the new business opportunities afforded by tourism.

The railways must take the credit for the rapid growth of both Cleethorpes and Mablethorpe in the nineteenth century, but what about now? Cleethorpes continues to be served by rail, but Mablethorpe lost its station and passenger line in 1970. The only train services in Mablethorpe nowadays (and very popular ones too) are the land train and the sand train. The first of these provides a regular service between the town and the Golden Sands complex, and as its name suggests, runs along the roads. By contrast, the second operates along the beach. Both are very popular with children (of all ages).

Access to the beach at the northern end of Mablethorpe requires a trip through the dunes. These are actually the southern tip of a five-mile stretch of sand dunes running as far as Saltfleet Haven and designated as a National Nature Reserve. Sand dunes are formed by the action of wind blowing over fine sandy beaches, pushing the tiny particles off the beach into mounds on top of existing vegetation or driftwood. Over time, the growth of grasses, thistles, sedges, even hawthorns, helps to stabilise the emerging dunes which then grow as strong winds pile more sand on top. Ironically it is the interest of humans in visiting dunes that causes the most damage to them. Dunes are fragile and even a group of people forging a track through sand dunes in search of a beach can lead to serious erosion. In some parts of the Mediterranean, for example, as much as three quarters of all sand dunes have been lost in the last thirty years. The consequences are potentially very serious. Dunes help to protect beaches from erosion and serve as a very effective flood barrier protecting inland homes and farms from damaging storm surges.

Much of the resort of Mablethorpe itself is man-made and has only existed for a hundred years or so. The dunes give the appearance of being a natural phenomenon that has always been there, so it may come as something of a surprise to learn that some of these aren't much older and the oldest of them all have only been there for around 800 years.

Dune management systems include the installation of dedicated walkways taking visitors across established dunes via boarded paths. Also chicken wire is frequently used to good effect as a framework for helping plants establish firm and stable roots. When visiting the Saltfleetby – Theddlethorpe Dunes National Nature Reserve, please take note of all signage – information is given for your safety AND in the interests of the long-term health of the dunes themselves.

Skegness has dune worries too. From Seacroft south as far as the Wash, Gibraltar Point Nature Reserve includes several square miles of spectacular dunes, much of which is now threatened. The problem has been caused by the successful installation of sea defences for Skegness itself, apparently. It seems that the energy from longshore drift that would previously have battered away at Skegness is now having a detrimental effect on the dunes to the south. Significant damage has already been done, but a new project involving the uprooting of buckthorn to be replaced with sturdier dune grasses is hoped to prevent further erosion and encourage more wildlife to inhabit the dunes.

As for beaches, Skegness boasts a long, wide sandy beach somewhat crudely bisected by the remains of what was once a rather grand pier. Those that know Skegness well will have seen how the beach has changed considerably since the addition of rock armour to bolster the sea defences in the 1990's. For the rest of us, there is a long low promenade to enjoy with plenty of clean sand and spectacular views up and down the coast as well as out to sea.

The pier is in a bit of a sorry state these days. At 129 yards long and little more than a few feet above the beach it is a far cry from the original t-shaped structure that opened to the public in 1881. At the time it was the fourth longest pier in the whole of England and featured a large concert hall at its head. The *Lincolnshire Chronicle* called it *"magnificent"* and reported *"thousands of visitors surging backwards and forwards"* on its opening day. Magnificent it most definitely was, at over 600 yards long with the invitation of steamboat trips to the Wash and Norfolk from the end of the pier for those seeking something more adventurous than musical entertainment. But, more of this later.

The beach itself has always offered visitors a miscellany of entertainment opportunities. On Whit Monday, 1881, the day Skegness Pier first opened to the public, the *Grantham Journal* reported that the beach also offered such amusements as *"donkey and pony riding"* and *"throwing for cocoa nuts"*. Donkey rides are still available for much of the year, and fairground attractions including at least one coconut shy are in an abundance throughout Skegness and the surrounding area. A somewhat newer attraction is the Skegness Beach Race – a motocross weekend festival held in the autumn each year. Crowds in excess of 20,000 flock to Skegness to watch solo riders, quad bikes and sidecar events on purpose-sculpted beach courses.

As we will discover elsewhere in this guide, Lincolnshire boasts mile after mile of very fine beaches. The three seaside giants attract the main crowds, but as will be revealed, there are plenty of excellent alternatives if you are prepared to wander a little from the beaten track.

Further Reading:

http://www.rspb.org.uk/discoverandenjoynature/seenature/reserves/guide/f/freistonshore/about.aspx

http://www.lincstrust.org.uk/reserves/saltfleetby-theddlethorpe-dunes

C is for Chemistry Sets – of the very, very large variety

Approaching the Brocklesby Interchange on the drive to Grimsby along the A180 the skyline to the north of the road is increasingly dominated by large steel chimneys. I once wondered why there should be a flame coming out of the top of one of them. Was something amiss? Was valuable energy simply going to waste? Then I read *Five Past Midnight in Bhopal* by Dominique Lapierre and Javier Moro. The authors carefully retell the compelling, horrifying and shameful story of the 1984 disaster at the Union Carbide pesticide plant in Bhopal, India that led to the deaths of thousands and injuries to over half a million people.

Reading the book taught me that these long, tall, pencil-thin chimneys were actually flare towers and that they serve a critical purpose. In the event of any form of gas leak from a chemical plant, the flare towers purpose is to burn off any potentially dangerous substance, thus rendering the gas harmless. What happened with such tragic consequences at Bhopal, did so partly because the flare tower was not in operation at the time of a catastrophic leak of highly toxic gas.

Lincolnshire had a chemical disaster of its own in 1974. Nypro UK had a large facility at Flixborough near Scunthorpe producing around 50,000 tons of Caprolactam every year. You may never have heard of it, but, without it, your toothbrush would have no bristles, your violin would probably be stringless and your surgeon would not be able to close your wound with sutures. Shortly before 5pm on Saturday 1st June 1974 following the escape of large quantities of hot cyclohexane a massive fuel-air explosion destroyed the entire plant and much of the surrounding area. Fires burnt for ten days. The explosion was heard in Grimsby and Hull, more than thirty miles away. Homes in Scunthorpe, more than three miles from the explosion, suffered damage from the blast. If we can be thankful of anything about a disaster that killed 28, at least it happened on a Saturday when only 72 people were on site. Only 8 people escaped injury.

The flare towers that can be seen on the approach to Grimsby belong to a pair of oil refineries straddling the main railway line adjacent to the villages of North and South Killingholme. The Lindsey Oil Refinery operated by Total and the Humber Refinery managed by Phillips 66 process almost half a million barrels of oil between them – every day! Imagine 30 Olympic-sized swimming pools full of crude oil and you're about there. Perhaps, more significantly for local communities, the refineries provide employment for almost 1000 people. Furthermore, the crude oil itself is pumped via underground pipes from large storage tanks near Tetney. Oil arrives in large tankers and is transferred offshore via the Tetney Monobuoy located in the Humber Estuary. This in turn is connected to the Tetney Oil Terminal by pipeline. The Monobuoy, by the way, is relatively easy to spot from somewhere like Cleethorpes. Just look out to sea, a little to the South of Spurn Point, for a bright yellow structure.

It is difficult to assess the impact of the two refineries in terms of total employment. As well as the 1000 or so directly employed at Lindsey and Humber, many of their products are shipped out of the country via the nearby Port of Immingham, which also handles oil and gas products on behalf of the two refineries. Those in charge of these young *"twins"* soon realised that they required so much *"food"* that a pair of gas-fired power stations were required nearby. These in turn provide much-needed jobs for many people living nearby. A conservative estimate is that between three and five thousand of North-East Lincolnshire's coastal population depend on the petro-chemical industry for their livelihoods.

Talking of Gas, another large plant at Theddlethorpe, just to the north of Mablethorpe processes and distributes around 10% of the United Kingdom's gas to households and industry. You'd be forgiven for not noticing it, even though the southern end of it is less than 150 yards from the Golden Sands holiday complex off Quebec Road in Mablethorpe. The gas comes from over 20 fields beneath the North Sea, many of them possessing somewhat unusual names like Valkyrie, Vampire and Audrey. Each field consists of one or more offshore platforms. The Audrey Field, for example comprises four platforms. Many of these are unmanned, but others provide employment for local people prepared to endure some of the harshest conditions possible. As of May 2016, the future of the

Theddlethorpe Gas Terminal and many of the North Sea Gas Fields connected to it is in doubt – competition from cheaply imported gas apparently causing economists to question the longer-term viability of these Lincolnshire coast landmarks. In the last decade the UK has moved from being virtually self-reliant to importing almost half of all gas used. Many are hoping that closure threats from the owners amount to nothing more than hot air.

How much gas does Theddlethorpe handle? According to Phillips66, up to 34 million cubic metres every day. What does that much gas look like? Remember the airship *Hindenburg*? You could fill that up 170 times over. If you are too young to know about airships, perhaps it helps to know that the same amount of gas could be used to fill the Royal Albert Hall every day for a year.

Of course, change is inevitable, and we are living in times where rapid, often unexpected change is commonplace. So perhaps it is worth reflecting for a moment on some of the "lost" industries of the Lincolnshire coastline. The area between Grimsby and Immingham, sometimes known as the South Humber Bank contains long stretches of largely undeveloped land prior to the nineteenth century. The industrial revolution and rapid urbanisation led to the construction of millions of new buildings throughout the British Isles. An abundance of readily-available clay along the banks of the Humber estuary led to what Neil Wright in his book *Lincolnshire Towns and Industry 1700 – 1914* described as a *"substantial industry"*. In the second half of the nineteenth century the number of brickyards operating along the Humber bank trebled and gave employment to hundreds of men. From an engineering point of view, bricks were ideal building materials, being relatively easy to obtain, light to work with and being suitable for a wide variety of construction styles and methods. They also afforded better insulation than timber and were far less expensive than stone. But there was another reason why bricks returned to favour after 1850 – the abolition of the Brick Tax.

During the reign of King George III, the seven-year-long American War of Independence had placed enormous strains on British finances. A year after the war ended, a tax on brick production was introduced to claw back some of the deficit. Initially set at 4 shillings per 1000 bricks, manufacturers quickly found a way to minimise the effect – they made bricks bigger – much bigger. The government responded almost immediately by setting a standard size for brick production and raising the levy to 5 shillings and 10 pence per 1000 bricks in 1805. By today's standards that still might not sound like a lot of money, but consider for example the building of Grimsby's iconic dock tower in 1851 – a year after the brick tax was abolished. With an estimated one million bricks made from clay excavated nearby to develop the docks area, the saving to the developers amounted to over £250.

Next time you take a stroll around any older looking settlement, take note of the brick sizes. Much larger than standard and you are probably looking at a building dating between 1780 and 1800, much smaller and the house is almost certainly even older.

Having passed over one of the Lincolnshire Coast's most memorable man-made landmarks, lets return and give it a closer look.

Further Reading:

B. Mummery, Immingham and the Great Central Legacy, History Press (1999)

N. Wright, Lincolnshire Towns and Industry 1700 – 1914, Lincoln (1982)

D is for a Dock Tower to Climb and a Diamond Jubilee Clock Tower to admire

Before we examine Lincolnshire's tallest building more closely I should mention that it is a long way short of being the tallest structure in the county. That honour goes to the Belmont TV transmission mast near Donnington on Bain, which at 1,153 feet comes in at almost four times the height of Grimsby's Dock Tower.

Grimsby's most notable landmark was completed in 1852 and is architecturally fashioned on Siena's Torre del Mangia, the clock tower adjacent to the Palazzo Pubblico in the city's main square. Grimsby can claim to have a taller tower – at 309 feet high it is 20 feet taller than Siena's tower, but Siena wins hands down in terms of age. Construction of the Grimsby Dock Tower was completed in 1852, some 504 years after the Torre Del Mangia.

Which is the best tower? I suppose that might depend to some extent on whether you hail from Lincolnshire or Tuscany, but as a neutral I will plump for the Dock Tower. Here are my reasons:

1. Siena's tower is largely decorative – a structural equal (in height at least) to the city's cathedral, built to symbolise equality between church and state. The dock tower had a material function. Inside it was a 30,000-gallon reservoir used to provide hydraulic power for the docks machinery nearby.

2. The Dock Tower was a single design and build, albeit modelled on Siena's tower, whereas the Tuscan monument features a marble loggia at its crest which was added four years after completion of the main brick tower.

3. Both towers survived intense bombing campaigns during World War II, but Grimsby's tower also withstood attempts by the British Government to demolish it in the belief that the Luftwaffe were using it as a landmark to help them target other English cities including Manchester and Liverpool. It is believed the Germans deliberately avoided bombing the tower as it was such a useful landmark for them. Following the war a

bronze plaque was placed on the west wall with the dedication "A tribute to those who swept the seas" to honour the many men involved in minesweeper work in the years 1939 – 1949.

4. Grimsby Dock Tower requires much more of an effort to climb. The original hydraulic lift is no longer in use and so visitors must climb a spiral staircase. The same is true of the Torre Del Mangia – some 400 or so steps to the top, but it is not that for that effort I decided Grimsby wins again. Siena's tower is open to visitors pretty much all year round, for a small admission charge, whereas Grimsby's dock tower is only open once or twice a year and then visitor numbers are carefully controlled, so access really is a rare privilege.

5. The view. Climb the dock tower and you can see the docks, the rest of Grimsby, as far south as Cleethorpes, Hull and the Humber Bridge and across the Humber to Spurn Point. All you can see from the Torre Del Mangia is the City of Siena and rolling Tuscan hills and countryside. (OK, perhaps it's a draw on this point).

6. Grimsby's tower is genuinely unique in that the power system concealed within its walls is believed to be the only application of William Armstrong's hydraulic technology of its kind whereas the Siena tower has several imitators including the Joseph Chamberlain Memorial Clock Tower at the University of Birmingham and no fewer than three replicas in the United States. Also, in Madrid the main building of the Spanish business and law school is topped with a clock tower modelled on the Torre Del Mangia.

The dock tower is an engineering marvel. Built on a base less than 30 feet square, it was the product of the imagination of architect James William Wild. A native of Lincoln, Wild had spent several years travelling through the Mediterranean countries, the middle east and Egypt prior to accepting the commission to construct the Great Grimsby Hydraulic Tower. (The larger docks project was in the hands of James Rendel and William Armstrong).

Legend has it that the tower is built on foundations of cotton wool. Although this is untrue, I can reveal the source of the myth. Digging footings so close to the sea is always challenging and this project was no exception. Excavations repeated filled with water until an ingenious solution was found. Someone reputedly mentioned that a nearby warehouse was holding several hundred bails of wool and that perhaps these might be used to soak up all the water that many days of bailing had been unable to remove. The plan worked but what was not recorded was whether the sodden wool bails were subsequently removed or if the hardcore footings were simply laid on top. In 1931 an earthquake offshore (at Dogger Bank) shook several buildings in Grimsby, including the tower, but it stood unscathed – many at the time claiming the cotton wool foundations had cushioned the effects of tremors felt as far away as Ireland.

Prince Albert had visited Grimsby to lay a foundation stone commemorating the start of this mammoth building programme. In October 1854, he returned, this time accompanying his wife, Queen Victoria, to survey the finished project and to officially open the docks and tower (two years after operational work had begun). The *Hull Advertiser and Exchange Gazette* revealed the extraordinary steps taken by the local authorities to ensure the royal party had a safe and satisfactory visit. The entire tower was painted white *"in the interior from top to bottom"* and decorated with *"white, pink and blue drapery"*. Doors had been painted white and blue. Even the wooden lift (described in those days as a carriage) didn't escape, being *"lined with scarlet cloth and covered on the outside with pink and white and blue calico"*. At the top, the viewing gallery had been carpeted in a *"very superb crimson"* and a seat *"with magnificent scarlet velvet cushions"* had been installed for the comfort and convenience of the royal party.

Nowadays, the tower is largely an empty shell. The water tanks and operating mechanisms are long gone as is the lift machinery. Occasional visits are possible from time to time and even though the building has great potential as a tourist attraction, the costs involved in complying with health and safety regulations have prevented any development works in that regard.

Our second tower is in Skegness and is no less prominent a local landmark despite being just 56 feet tall. Built between 1898 and 1899 to commemorate Victoria's Diamond Jubilee it was funded entirely by public subscription. These days the "jolly fisherman" is generally considered to be the icon of Skegness – indeed, his statue stands beside the clock tower on Lumley Road, but the tower came first by a decade.

The Diamond Jubilee Clock Tower was designed by a Liverpool architect, Edmund Winter but built by a local man – Bostonian W H Parker.

When the Countess of Scarborough officially declared the tower open in August 1899 there must have been many breathing sighs of relief. Just five months earlier, emergency meetings had taken place to secure the final £150 needed (of a total cost of £550) to complete the project.

On the first day of April 2009 the Skegness Standard caused a brief outcry in the local area when it reported that the tower was to be demolished and re-erected inside a museum. Being the 1st of April, perhaps its readers should have thought twice before taking up arms in protest. It was, of course, nothing more than a hoax.

As a major seafront landmark, the tower has subsequently lent its name to several other notable buildings in Skegness. The Tower Cinema was built in the early 1920's by local entrepreneur Fred Clements and was originally intended to be a theatre. However, being the only cinema in the area equipped for sound, it quickly established itself as a popular venue. It was bombed and damaged badly in January 1941, leading to major demolition and rebuilding work after the war. The bombing from a lone German aircraft resulted in the death of a café owner nearby and several near misses. This is all the more remarkable given that the cinema had been filled with Saturday afternoon matinee-goers and the neighbouring streets had been milling with shoppers. The clock tower also sustained some damage but was promptly repaired.

To tell the story of Tower Gardens and its pavilion requires a short detour to look at a man who invested heavily in Skegness as a Victorian seaside resort – the Earl of Scarborough.

Richard George Lumley was born at Tickhill Castle near Doncaster on 7th May 1813. He inherited the family titles following the death of his cousin, the eighth Earl in October 1856. Along with the Earldom came land, an awful lot of land – including much of Skegness and its surroundings which had been part of the Scarborough estate since 1723.

Lumley had no need to find ways to earn more money but he saw that Skegness with its ten mile stretch of wide sandy beaches was a development opportunity too good to miss. He invested in the new railway programme, built roads, homes, hotels and largely reshaped Skegness as a seaside resort.

Perhaps the "Scarborough" family tree might help to explain some of the road and street names near the seafront. Lumley Road and Lumley Avenue require no further explanation. But where Ida Road, Lilian Road, Algitha Road and Sibell Road come from? The Earl's wife, Frederica bore four daughters – so now you know. (By the way, Lilian and Sibell Road featured in the original plans but no longer exist, and Prince George Street was subsequently added between Algitha Road and Lumley Road). Also, she was grand-daughter to the fifth Duke of Rutland which also explains where Rutland Road got its name. Similarly, the Earl himself through his maternal line was descended from Marcus Beresford, 1st Earl of Tyrone, hence Beresford Avenue. Drummond was Frederica's maiden name – honoured with Drummond Road running parallel to the sea front.

Alongside Lumley Road is Sandbeck Avenue which has a similar ancestry. The Earl appointed his Land Agent Henry Vivian Tippet to handle his affairs. Tippet's residence at the time (although he later moved to Skegness) was Sandbeck Park near Rotherham. Under Tippet's direction the Earl funded the pier, grand parade, pleasure gardens (and the aforementioned pavilion), public baths and many more facilities all designed to draw in the tourists.

A novel way of collecting revenue featured in the early years of Skegness as a holiday resort. The Earl had significant investment in the railways and since most visitors arrived in Skegness by train, it was decided to include admission to all of the attractions in the ticket price (with Scarborough receiving a share, of course). The concept of unlimited "rides" from a single ticket is now a familiar one, used by most, if not all theme parks. Perhaps Skegness was the first theme park?

Returning to our main theme – the pleasure gardens and pavilion opened to the public in 1879, six years after the first regular railway service commenced. The pavilion offered a large function space, indoor facilities for tea and dancing and, as was increasingly popular in Victorian times, became the place to be seen. Over the decades, the pavilion has undergone many transformations including being an American Diner for a while, as well as being an auction house, a factory, a public house a scout hut and a nursery. At this point in time it is a sad, derelict shell, in danger of falling down or being pulled down unless major investment can be found to generate new life into this iconic landmark.

As for the Clock Tower – its future is seemingly secure, recent problems with a covering of green algae have been sorted out and the tower stands proudly as one of the most prominent and memorable landmarks in Skegness.

Having considered a couple of landscape alterations made intentionally, let us consider awhile more natural phenomena and their effects on the coast.

Further Reading:

M. Davison, The Grimsby Dock Tower, History of Industry & Technology (1966)

W. Kime & K. Wilkinson, Skegness Past & Present, History Press (2011)

E is for Environmental Changes since Edwardian Times

The Skegness Clock Tower we just looked at stands in the middle of a roundabout connecting South Parade with Lumley Road. When the "*Grand Parade*" was being planned in the 1870's maps show that it was laid out to follow the coastline. The most revealing aspect of Henry Tippet's 1878 plan for "*the sea-bathing place*" is that the Parade featured six places where steps were to be laid out – directly onto the beach below.

Why is this little detail so remarkable? Look at Skegness now, some 138 years later. The Parade is still there, but where the steps to the beach had been planned is now developed land. In fact, so much developed land that a theatre, swimming pool, lifeboat station, model village, aquarium, several car parks and the pleasure beach amusements all now stand on what would then have been the beach.

Is this "new" land a new feature? Not at all. In fact, looking back some 500 years the coastline then pretty much followed the line now taken by the A52, Skegness to Wainfleet Road. Gibraltar Point did not exist and was in fact about four miles out to sea in those days! The coastline at Skegness itself has changed so much that if it's 600-yard-long pier had been built on the same spot two hundred years earlier – it would not have reached the sea! So, where does all this new land come from?

Some might look at the massive scale of erosion further north along the Holderness coast – 10 feet or more being lost annually in many places and assume that Lincolnshire is gaining land at the expensive of Yorkshire. This is not the case. In fact, most of the eroded Yorkshire coastline ends up being whipped around Spurn Point before being deposited on the inner bank of the peninsula – still in Yorkshire.

To help find the answer takes a closer examination of Lincolnshire's beaches. These are largely shallow in gradient and typically contain ridges and runnels (little valley-like hollows) that remain filled with shallow water at low tide. Looking at the direction the ridges follow helps to establish the dominant flow of the tides. In Lincolnshire, coastal ridges tend to be orientated to the South West. This tells us that the tidal flow is predominantly from the north east. Scientific studies have shown that most of deposits along the Lincolnshire coastline flowed out of the Humber estuary and therefore originated near the shores of the rivers that lead to the Humber – namely the Trent, Ouse and Ancholme Rivers. Somehow, I doubt that the members of Seacroft Golf Club to the south of Skegness would appreciate the thought that their course is laid out more on Yorkshire soil than Lincolnshire!

The situation in the proximity of Lincolnshire's resort towns is also strongly influenced by the siting and nature of man-made coastal defences. For example, at Cleethorpes the shore front sea walls protect the town, but erosion to the south near Humberston is some of the most severe in the whole of England – over 5 metres a year at times. Authorities have faced, and still face, difficult choices. Do they protect a town and its tourism trade at the expense of householders, farmers, caravan site owners and others whose land just a mile or two away could well disappear before their eyes in a matter of a few years? Thankfully, advances in science and engineering now mean that sea defences can be built that absorb energy rather than deflect it – which goes some way to solving the problem rather than moving it somewhere else.

Cleethorpes seafront is virtually unrecognisable from the view experienced by Walter White, Assistant Secretary of the Royal Society, in 1865. In his book *Eastern England From The Thames to The Humber* he described the view as he arrived in Cleethorpes for the first time:

> *"... red houses and a windmill crowning a bluff that seems to be the termination of a branch ridge running from the wolds to the Humber. Of this situation the village seems to be not a little proud, for of all the Lincolnshire watering places it alone can boast of a cliff."*

A Cliff?! In Cleethorpes? Not only a Cliff, but a Cliff Hotel standing on it too! But where and what became of both? The Cliff Hotel stood on the corner of Sea View Street and what is now the A1098 overlooking, as you might expect, the cliff. Some may remember it as *JD's Nightscene* but the entire building is long gone, with "*The Point*" standing imposingly on the same site. Edwardian picture postcards reveal the landscape to have already been sculpted as it is nowadays with a tram service operating along the main road and turnstile access to the beautifully laid out Pier Gardens invitingly opposite the hotel entrance.

Surely this isn't the same spot that out illustrious friend from the Royal Society described some forty years earlier? White's own words reveal the answer:

> *"From this modest elevation, which, as may be inferred from the term clee, is composed mostly of clay, the visitors who use it as their chief resort and lounging place can overlook the beach, and the breezy common; the strollers and donkeys; the cocklers, bathing machines and all that sails the water between the two shores."*

The clay cliff was, in fact, wearing away so rapidly that something dramatic was required to prevent the loss of Cleethorpes seafront buildings into the sea. Erosion of the cliff had first been identified as a problem by an earlier fellow of the Royal Society, Abraham de la Pryme who, almost two hundred years earlier had written with some alarm about successive tides tearing away pieces of the cliff the size of churches day after day.

De la Pryme believed Cleethorpes had the potential to rival or even surpass Grimsby as a major sea port, but only if the cliff could have been prevented from further damage by the erection of a large staith at the base of the cliff to enable shipping to dock safely. Little had been done to arrest the sea's progress by the time Walter White picked up the story. The Manchester, Sheffield and Lincolnshire Railway Company finally dealt with the problem, but when they acted, they did so with no shortage of style.

What was required involved two measures of protection. Something at the seafront to prevent further erosion, and, crucially, as engineers and surveyors had realised, something behind the seafront to prevent further crumbing and collapsing of the cliff top. Prince Albert Victor, the 21-year-old Duke of Clarence and Avondale (or plain "Eddy" to family and close friends) visited Cleethorpes at the beginning of July 1885 to *"inaugurate the picturesque High Cliff Garden"* as the *Morning Post* newspaper reported in London the following day. The newspaper established two motives behind the railway company's massive investment. Firstly *"to arrest the inroads of the sea"* and, secondly *"to afford means of healthful recreation and amusement to the inhabitants"*. As the newspaper continued with its report, the intention was to develop Cleethorpes potential for tourism *"associated with the gardens are a promenade and pier, which will greatly increase the attractions of Cleethorpe (sic) as a watering place."*

The results of two years' hard labours and a considerable sum of money was described enthusiastically by a reporter from the Sheffield Daily Telegraph who wrote:

"All along the most frequented part of the foreshore there stretches a magnificent sea-wall, rising six or eight feet above the height of normal spring tides, and enclosing a width of the old beach varying from 70 feet to 100 feet, which has been filled up and solidified level with the wall, making a broad, even surface, along the entire length of which is formed an imposing promenade, carriage drive and inner walk. The former rugged brow of the cliff, euphemistically termed the "Recreation Ground" is now a smiling garden, artistically laid out with due regard to the natural undulations of the ground, and planted with shrubs and flowers. The highest point, opposite Sea View Street is marked by a peculiar conical structure, built after an ancient fashion, with stones of all shapes and sizes designated " Ross Castle," the pile appearing at a short distance like some tower or castle of "ye olden time". Midway between the and the pier, on a lower terrace of ornamental grounds, has been built a handsome bathing establishment, in the Queen Anne style of architecture. To the right, looking from the beach and close to the pier is a conservatory for bedding plants. To the west of the pier the old sandy track from the Dolphin Hotel down to the beach, once known as the Folly Hole, and latterly as Sea Road, now a firm road in fact as well as in name, which after crossing the sea-wall, is extended by a gentle declivity to the level of the sands, with a paved carriage way and flagged side walks, which form a most convenient landing place for the various pleasure boats that ply for hire during the season. From the top of Sea road, and separated from it by a wall describing a shapely and rising curve, runs a substantial road up to the pier gates, and in the recess formed on the lower side of the wall, a suite

of rooms has been constructed. The scene landward from the pier head, or from the boats upon the water, instead of being somewhat colourless and dull, as aforetime, is now bright, animated, and refreshing, the white face of the sea wall, the moving throng on the promenade, the vivid green of the slopes, with the varied tints from the gardens, ornamented buildings and the Blue arcade furnishing a prospect quite as alluring as the seaward view from the shore."

With the inclusion of hot and cold salt and fresh water baths, a bandstand and a 200-yard long stretch of covered trading booths providing a sheltered route (as well as several opportunities to part with money) all the way to and from the railway station, the Manchester Courier felt able to congratulate the developers on achieving *"a large measure of success"*.

At this point you may be wondering why the word *"Edwardian"* appears in the title to this chapter?

Cleethorpes Victorian growth, stimulated largely out of economic interest, but with more than just a passing nod to environmental factors was repeated at Mablethorpe and Skegness. As each town grew and became increasingly crowded as a tourist resort into the early years of the twentieth century, room for expansion was sought largely along the "ribbon corridors" of the major, and sometimes minor, roads. Consequently, villages became towns and sometimes merged with neighbouring villages into larger settlements. This is a trend that has continued to the present day. So much so that, for example, it is now difficult to distinguish between Grimsby, Cleethorpes and Humberston – all of which were distinct territories a century ago. Perhaps the most striking example of this ribbon growth can be seen at Skegness. In Edwardian Lincolnshire, Skegness, Ingoldmells and Chapel St. Leonards were completely separate with miles of open countryside and undeveloped coastline between them. Nowadays it is possible to walk along the beach from "Chapel" to Ingoldmells before picking up Roman Bank and continuing all the way to the centre of Skegness – a journey of six miles – without seeing any undeveloped land along the way.

The Edwardian boom saw hundreds of large villas being constructed along main thoroughfares in the increasingly popular resorts, but then came the war years, the Spanish flu pandemic and global economic depression in the twenties. After this holiday homes would never be the same. Caravan parks, chalet homes and affordable bed and breakfast accommodation became the norm. One businessman's example typified the new approach to tourism. His name was Billy Butlin, and more of him will follow.

Firstly, though we must dig deep into the Fens of Lincolnshire.

Further Reading:

J. Wright, Skegness – Lincolnshire's Famous Seaside Resort, e-book (2016)

A. Dowling, Cleethorpes – The Creation of a Seaside Resort, Phillimore (2008)

F is for Fen: Flat, Flooded and home of the Fen-slodger

William Henry Wheeler, Surveyor to the Boston Corporation and Harbour Engineer, gave such a good description of a *"fen-slodger"* in an 1889 talk entitled The Fens of South Lincolnshire, that it bears repeating here. He called them:

"half amphibious beings who got their living by fishing and fowling, living in isolated spots in huts erected on the mounds scattered amongst the chain of lakes which were bordered with thick crops of weeds ... Although their condition was very miserable, they nevertheless enjoyed a sort of wild liberty amidst the watery wastes"

Wheeler explained how the reclamation of the marshy fen lands in the interests of intensive farming techniques was at odds with the lifestyles of these most hardy and peculiar of men whose *"gunning boat has had to give way to the plough and the steam thrashing machine."* He continued:

"The geese and the wild fowl have been displaced by oxen and sheep, and the swamp and the mere become one of the richest tracts of cultivated land in the kingdom, the home of an industrious, hard-working population, as law-abiding and contented as their predecessors (the slodgers) were lawless and wild."

To understand why all this was happening and the reasoning behind W.H. Wheeler's anti-slodger stance we need to dig a little deeper into the fens themselves.

In Wheelers own words can be found disputes over the rights to live and work in the fens going back hundreds of years. In fact, the problem can probably be traced back to the occupation of higher ground amongst the boggy lowlands by several groups of monks in the twelfth and thirteenth centuries. Wheeler noted:

"grants of land, and rights of fishing, fowling and turbary; which rights appear to have been considered of much value from the numerous disputes respecting them. On the banks of the Witham, twelve religious

houses were erected within the space of twenty miles. As these monasteries increased in size and importance they attracted numerous tenants, retainers and servants."

So it was the monks who obtained land grants and rights from the crown. These in turn established enclosures and effectively partitioned large areas of fenland to work for their own profit. Part of that income came from the sale of rights to independent tenants – the first slodgers.

It was always an uneasy relationship. The monasteries were eager to develop the rich highly fertile fenland with ever larger and more extensive drainage programmes and flood defence systems, while many of their tenants strove to maintain their households and feed their families by fishing and fowling in the flooded fens.

You may be wondering about that third right mentioned just now – turbary. This was an ancient order granting a tenant the right to cut peat or turf from a bog – in this case a fen. The cut sods of turf made excellent fuel to heat homes and power stoves. In some cases brine was extracted from the sodden turf to produce salt in sufficient quantities as to provide a reasonable trade.

The process of "enclosing" common land achieved two significant purposes for the crown. Firstly, it enabled the monarch to reward loyal subjects with the allocation of territory, and, secondly it provided a means for raising additional revenue through the collection of taxes. Matters probably came to a head in the reign of King James I. Once again, William Wheeler picks up the story:

"Orders were made for works to be carried out for the reclamation of the fens and taxes to be levied for cost of the same, and in default of the owners to pay these the fens were handed over to certain adventurers, who undertook to carry out the necessary banks, drains and sluices for the drainage of the fens."

Sir Anthony Thomas headed up the operation for the King between the Witham and the coast. The works took three years to complete, but within another seven years *"the disposed fenmen forcibly regained possession of the land"*.

In what is now known as the Black Sluice District, to the south of Boston, the Earl of Lindsey attempted to drain the unimaginatively titled "Lindsey Levels" around 1635. Wheeler noted *"the Earl and his fellow adventurers inclosed the Fens, built houses and farmsteads, and brought the land into cultivation"*. This lasted for three years until *"the fenmen destroyed the sluices"*.

It all boiled down to money in the end. The Fen slodgers wanted nothing more than to maintain a lifestyle going back hundreds of years. One of incredibly hard personal work with little gain other than to meet the needs of a family. On the other hand, entrepreneurs saw the fens as land from which a fortune could be had – at any price.

Wheeler, a Londoner, educated at King's College, represented the establishment, a long-time servant of parliament and an authority on land reclamation and drainage systems. To him, the slodgers would have been rebels, terrorists, a scourge, a thorn in the side of the developers. No doubt the slodgers, working the fens for generations had similar views about the people threatening their traditional way of life.

What was it about the Fens of Lincolnshire that led to such strong feelings? Perhaps Wheeler again gives us a clue by describing them as:

> *"an enormous tract of land (once) little better than a huge swamp …*
> *converted by the energy of man into one of the most productive districts*
> *of the country."*

More telling is the fact that although only 5% of all the agricultural land in England is officially graded as "excellent", almost the entire fenlands of Lincolnshire have been classified in the top category, accounting for half of the nation's premium farmland. This fact was not lost on the Romans who pushed steadily into the fens of Lincolnshire, Cambridgeshire and Norfolk, forcing out the early Britons where they could before making the first attempts at draining these oft-flooded lowlands.

Fens are naturally fertile. Their biology is complex, but essentially result from decaying vegetation and woodland, sodden by both salt and fresh water, frozen and thawed repeatedly, abraded by advancing and retreating glaciers and populated by thousands, possibly millions of different lifeforms – many of them unique to this habitat. Archaeologists have unearthed remains of walruses and whales in the clay layers beneath wild oxen and wolves preserved in the peat bogs.

Nowadays the Fens are home to thousands of the most modern, intensive and productive farms to be found anywhere in the developed world. Produce ranges from poultry to pot plants, cereals to celery and potatoes to pak choi. Sadly, Cranberry Fen at Friskney, no longer produces cranberries. John Marius Wilson's *Imperial Gazetteer of England and Wales* published around 1872 explained the demise of cranberry farming:

"From 2, 000 to 4, 000 pecks of cranberries also were annually gathered from Cranberry fen; but, after the drainage of the tract, the gathering of them almost ceased."

How many cranberries would that have been? About 30 cubic metres – more than enough to give a million people a good serving of cranberry sauce alongside a roast turkey dinner. Turkeys, by the way, are also farmed in the Lincolnshire Fens!

Development of the fens is still very much a work in progress, but if specific credit is due to one individual – Cornelius Vermuyden who would have to be the prime candidate. Vermuyden, a Dutchman, had served his engineering apprenticeship in his native Holland, where land reclamation and drainage techniques were already well advanced compared with Britain. By the age of thirty he was working on fen drainage projects in Lincolnshire and at thirty four he received a knighthood from King Charles I (largely for his work draining Hatfield Chase – at that time in Lincolnshire, now part of South Yorkshire). Perhaps most noteworthy of his innovations was the concept of "washes" – dedicated sections of land allowed, even forced, to flood, holding excess water during bad weather, so as to protect delicate farmland. This principle is being used in the present day by the governments Environment Agency as a strategy to protect communities from flood waters as climate change brings more frequent extreme weather systems to our shores.

Vermuyden's initial legacy was to create great swathes of lowland that regularly flooded. He and his contemporaries had not understood that draining peat bogs would cause the dry peat to shrink to such an extent that land levels dropped considerably. The industrial revolution and the development of steam-driven pumps remedied this situation – two centuries of some of the most challenging farming conditions imaginable later. Much of the Dutchman's engineering would be considered naïve by todays standards and many regard the conduct of his fellow "adventurers" as unacceptable (the use of prisoners of war for labour and the forced removal of traditional independent farmers from their homes, are just two examples). However, without Vermuyden and his contemporaries it is possible that the fens of Eastern England would not be what they are today.

Prospects for the fens are pretty bleak. Sea levels are predicted to rise by a metre before the end of this century. That may not seem much, but this, together with an increase in both the intensity and frequency of storm surges as a result to global warming combine to threaten the stability and future prospects for this delicate section of Lincolnshire's coastline. A story from 2013 illustrates the fragility of this area. The Lincolnshire Wildlife Trust look after a large section of coastal Fens, dunes and wetlands between Skegness and the Wash (we will find out more of their work in this area in the next chapter). A massive storm surge in December 2013 caused so much flood damage to their visitors centre at Gibraltar Point that it had to be demolished. The new building – the trust themselves quite fairly describe it as *"spectacular"* - has been designed to be as future proof as possible by raising it on stilts well above the two-feet deep flood waters that ruined the old centre. These measures come at a high price. The costs of demolition and replacing flood damaged items are not known, but the new build alone cost considerably more than a million pounds!

Further Reading:

M. W. Barley, Lincolnshire and the Fens, EP Publishing (1972)

W. H. Wheeler, A History of the Fens of South Lincolnshire, Cambridge (2013)

Also, free to read online at:
https://archive.org/details/cu31924014023893

G is for Gibraltar ... a Point to Prove

As we have seen already, the Lincolnshire coastline to the south of Skegness bears little resemblance to the shore line of a couple of hundred years ago.

Gibraltar Point owes its existence to a combination of factors – accretion and land reclamation, both of which we have already dipped into so we will focus our interests here on the point itself with just a passing reference to its history.

The Steeping River is actually the River Lymn, by another name, as it takes its final meandering (and often man-made) route to the sea, between Wainfleet and Gibraltar Point. Once a regular route for shipping heading to dock at Wainfleet, it has suffered from centuries of silting to the extent that the only human traffic along its waters nowadays is that of a sailing club, based just a couple of hundred yards from the sea. Wainfleet Haven was once a major port, a centre for the export of wool and grain.

Since at least the twelfth century salt extraction has been a major business in this area. Now long gone, the main evidence of its existence consists of a pair of large mounds beside the A52 between Wainfleet and Friskney. These were once *salterns* – spoil heaps – from the extraction process but their height also made them suited for the siting of beacons to guide shipping into the nearby port, avoiding the treacherous sandbanks offshore. Several other smaller mounds, many only apparent from aerial photography point to a history of salt production on a massive scale.

Entering and leaving the port of Wainfleet invariably involved manoeuvring shipping around the dangerous waters off Gibraltar Point. Newspapers have reported countless wrecks – the earliest I could find were a pair of shipping disasters in 1791, a Dutch vessel carrying a cargo of corn was lost early in the year and the Robert and Mary *"laden with tiles"* sank as it approached Wainfleet in December of the same year.

The geography of Gibraltar Point is complex but one thing is very straightforward – it is nothing like its namesake in the Mediterranean. The rock of Gibraltar is just that, a limestone promontory rising to over 400 metres. Gibraltar Point is the southernmost tip of a nature reserve comprising a pair of parallel sand dune ridges sandwiching a half-kilometre wide salt marsh. Gibraltar is also a nature reserve, most famous for a large colony of macaque monkeys, whereas Gibraltar Point is home to skylarks, sanderlings, pipits, snipes, terns and redshanks. The saltmarshes are covered with a carpet of sea lavender in the summer months, while the dunes with their grasses are home to dozens of species of insects. With inshore freshwater lagoons and ponds there is something for every nature lover.

The new visitors centre mentioned in the last chapter has been built beside the old coastguard station. Built in 1859, it saw operational service until the 1920's. When sold by auction at the Lion Hotel, Skegness in April 1926 it wasn't the two-bedroomed bungalow or the enclosed half-acre of land that attracted potential purchasers. Even the attached lookout tower with views to sea on a clear day of over fifteen miles wasn't the prime motivator for buying the lot. The auctioneer pointed out that the nearby sandbanks were home to a large colony of seals and that any buyer might make a comfortable living by killing and selling them. The going rate in those days before conservation and protection orders were in place was ten shillings per "nose". Whether this was a determining factor or not, we do not know, but the purchaser paid five times the opening bid price.

One of the early coastguard men at Gibraltar Point was David Hull. How, in July 1872, a coastguard tragically lost his life due to the theft of chickens is a story that must be told. What the Grantham Journal described as a "shocking circumstance" began with the allegation that several Dutch sailors had stolen thirteen couple of chickens" from the grounds of a cottage occupied by Ellerby Smalley. Police Constable Smalley's investigations led to the coastguard putting out the lifeboat in pursuit of the Dutchmen. Their vessel was boarded but no trace of the missing fowl was found. On the return journey, "a sudden squall of wind upset the boat" plunging all the occupants into the deep waters of the North Sea. As they drifted away from shore with the outgoing tide, all the crew members were saved – except poor David Hull who was last seen clinging to the upturned lifeboat.

These days most of those venturing to Gibraltar Point do so with the prospect of viewing some of the many different species of wildlife that inhabit the area. Sadly, this has not always been the case. Those that took guns to the Point in search of ducks and other fowl did not always return home unscathed though. In 1946, two teenagers, Gordon Kirk and Alvis Blanchard left Skegness to go hunting wild duck at Gibraltar Point. Blanchard somehow discharged his gun by accident resulting in an injury to his unfortunate friend.

A couple of years later four more Skegness lads took themselves off to Gibraltar Point in search of war souvenirs. The trip would cost two of them their lives as *The Lincolnshire Standard & Boston Guardian* reported. Whilst filling their pockets with cartridge cases and flares, one of the boys saw *"a round object in the sand, with only the screw part showing"*. Twelve-year-old Philip Judd and Neville Hull (11) dug the object out with their bare hands but despite warnings from their friends to *"throw it away"*, the two boys continued to explore their find until a deafening explosion took both their lives in an instant. An inquest found that the boys had dug up a mortar bomb, just one of several potentially lethal devices left behind by the army who had used the area as a training site during the war years.

Even if you have never been to Gibraltar Point, it is likely that you have unwittingly seen it. In 1954, filming for a key scene in The Dam Busters movie took place there. The film tells the story of *Operation Chastise* – a plan to attack dams in the Ruhr and Eder valleys. Barnes Wallis conducted tests of his bouncing bomb in the Thames Estuary but the film makers found the area to be too developed by the mid 50's and so selected the wild unspoilt Lincolnshire coast to "stand in". At the time, an RAF station was in operation at nearby Wainfleet, facilities to accommodate and cater for seventy or co cast members and crew were to be had just up the road in Skegness so Gibraltar Point came to be used to film a famous scene where the bombs were dropped from too high an altitude causing them to break up on impact and for Wallis (played by Sir Michael Redgrave) to respond to an RAF commander *"I am afraid you must think me rather a fraud"*. Of course, in the movie, and in real life, Wallis went on to perfect the technique resulting in the breaching of The Möhne and Edersee Dams.

Your best chance of catching sight of a few stars at Gibraltar Point is go to there after sundown, but you are likely to see several species of migrating seabirds including (during winter months) Oystercatchers, Red Knots and the Bar-tailed godwit (a bird capable of non-stop flights in excess of 6,000 miles – somewhat more than the RAF Lancaster bombers used in the Dam Busters raid!).

Gibraltar Point is a fantastic place for a day trip. For those coming to the Lincolnshire coast with a longer stay in mind thoughts now turn to holiday accommodation.

Further Reading:

J. D. Golicher, Gibraltar Point Walkabout Guide, Pamphlet (1972)

For regular updates from the bird observatory visit:

http://gibraltarpointbirdobservatory.blogspot.co.uk/

H is for Holiday Homes, the Humberston Fitties and Huts by the Beach

Whilst researching Gibraltar Point for the previous chapter, my attention was caught by the following newspaper advertisement, published in the 30th April 1938 edition of the *Grantham Journal*:

For Sale, Converted BUS CARAVAN

at Gibraltar Point, Skegness, large

and roomy, 2 rooms, furnished:

£10 the lot.

The advertisement did not identify the model of "BUS CARAVAN" for sale. What can be stated with some confidence is that this would have been one of the very early forerunners of the increasingly popular modern-day motorhomes. In some cases, car manufacturers turned out extremely stylish motor caravans based on popular coach-built saloon cars such as the Morris Oxford. Others were less impressive in their appearance. Which would you prefer – a car that you could live in for your holidays, or a caravan that you could drive around? Most of the motor caravans of this period resembled a caravan with a windscreen and a driver's seat, unfortunately.

A year later, this advertisement appeared in the *Scunthorpe Evening Telegraph*:

For Sale, Furnished Bungalow

Humberston Fitties, near beach, £70

Before we consider the "*Humberston Fitties*", perhaps it is worth comparing the value of these two items for sale. Average UK household income in the 1930's was around £165, so purchasing the bungalow required roughly five months' wages for a typical family, whereas the "*bus caravan*" could be bought for about four weeks' earnings. In the same newspaper column, other bungalows were on the market at three times the *"Fitties"* price, so what was it about these properties that made them more affordable?

The word *"Fitties"* is used throughout Lincolnshire wherever there are salt marshes – hardly prime land for the development of holiday accommodation you might think? In fact, the only newspaper mentions of the Humberston Fitties I could find prior to the outbreak of World War I were all connected with sheep farming. The reason for the development of buildings in this prime coastal pasture land can be found by looking out to sea.

Just off the coast can be seen Haile Sand Fort, a remarkable piece of engineering, rising almost 60 feet above the water with a diameter of over 80 feet. The fort was planned to protect the Humber estuary entrance from German invaders but took over four years to complete, by which time the war was over. At one time, up to 4,000 soldiers, mostly belonging to the Manchester Regiment, were stationed along this stretch of coastline, primarily to defend Grimsby, Cleethorpes and the like from the threat of German attackers, but also to assist with the construction of any new fortifications.

Many of the military men were billeted in the towns themselves – in one case with catastrophic and tragic consequences, as will be retold later. Several groups were stationed in the surrounding countryside and along the coast. In some cases, tents gave way to the erection of wooden huts, or to the commandeering and relocating of old railway carriages. There were even stories of trams and buses being converted into temporary homes for soldiers. Quite quickly, the Humberston Fitties became a bustling and rapidly expanding community, albeit, a military one.

After the war, the Manchester Regiment moved out, but most of their buildings remained and became instantly popular with holidaymakers and day-trippers. For a while the Fitties was home to a ramshackle mix of wooden huts, caravans, buses and decaying rolling stock. Some became holiday homes for soldiers returning with their families, while others became bases for weekend fishing trips, bird spotting expeditions and other reasons to escape to the seaside.

As popular as they'd become the Humberston Fitties couldn't escape one simple fact – Fitties are marshes. Marshes are wet and prone to flooding. As the occupants frequently found out. By 1935, most of the original huts had been replaced with more appropriate flood-resistant chalets built on stilts or equipped with wheels – ready for a quick move as water levels rose. At this time, too, the authorities had realised the site needed to be regulated, as much as for health and safety reasons as for the opportunity to raise revenue from taxation. So, in 1938, control passed to the local council – just in time for the next World War.

For the war years, the chalets were taken into military hands and used as barracks for soldiers undertaking training prior to active service. The next big change for the Fitties also involved a large military operation – what became known as Lincolnshire's Dunkirk. On the weekend of 31st January – 1st February 1953 the Lincolnshire Coast experienced a storm and flooding on an unprecedented scale. Dozens lost their lives and thousands were evacuated from their homes. At Humberston, the sea destroyed many of the chalets, badly damaged others – even lifting up a few before depositing them several yards away in a state unfit for any further habitation.

The legacy of the '53 floods is that chalets no longer have a sea view. Flood defences now include a large raised sand ridge that affords good storm protection but does detract from the romance of a secluded holiday cottage by the seashore. Also, new regulations prohibit lease holders from staying overnight during the months of January and February.

At the last count, there were just over 300 chalets still in some state of use – including a few that can be dated back prior to the 1953 disaster. Some are quite luxurious, spacious and available for private holiday rentals. Just a stone's throw from one of the widest expanses of sandy beach in England makes them an attractive proposition for someone looking for a traditional seaside holiday.

A little further down the road at Sutton-on-Sea (25 miles to be precise), can be found a different kind of seaside tradition – the beach hut. Their forerunner was the portable bathing machine – an essential piece of apparatus in the more modest days of Georgian and Victorian England when gentleman and ladies would not wish to be seen unsuitably attired prior to a dip in the sea. (In fact, King George III is known to have used one as long ago as 1789.) As habits changed so these "machines" retreated to more permanent bases often alongside promenades or sea walls and swapped their sea legs (wheels) for solid foundations.

Nowadays, a beach hut is a prime asset, particularly if it comes with dedicated seafront car parking so it is not surprising to find that they change hands very quickly – even with prices of £15,000 or more for a hut often no bigger than 12 feet square. Most huts come with very basic facilities – a socket or two to power a kettle and maybe a toaster, a sink (and if you are lucky, water on tap) and somewhere to sit. If you are thinking these brightly coloured structures would make a beautiful holiday home, forget it. As a general rule, local authorities prohibit overnight stays.

Sutton-on-Sea and neighbouring Sandilands are home to several rows of beach huts, some in private ownership with others under the control of the local council. At present, the future of at least some of them is in considerable doubt. East Lindsey District Council, under pressure to squeeze services have considered pulling a row of 27 huts down rather than pursue costly, but essential, renovations. However, a resident's association stepped in and, in the short term at least, the huts remain available for public hire.

The people of Sutton-on-Sea really care about their beach huts – in fact, they run their own Beach Hut Owners Association and provide a patrol and report service for all hut owners with a stated aim to *"maintain and preserve (beach huts) for the enjoyment of future generations"*. Sutton even hosts a weekend beach hut festival every summer featuring music, dancing, trade stalls and traditional beach games.

Thumb through a pile of old picture postcards and you'll see the habit of painting beach huts and bathing machines in bright colours goes back a long way. No one can be sure how this started but given that bathing machines were available for public hire and there were often dozens of them on a single stretch of beach, a splash of strong colour could make one stand out. At Sutton-on-Sea, those in public ownership tend to be painted in primary colours while the privately-owned huts are more varied and often feature pastels and mixed colours as well as more than a handful of "themed" huts – I'll not spoil the surprise – take a walk along the promenade and look for yourselves!

The most prolific provider of homes for holidays along the Lincolnshire Coast must have been Billy Butlin. His first UK holiday camp opened at Skegness in 1936, nine years after Butlin had begun what was to be a lifelong association with the east coast resort when he established an amusement park featuring slides, stalls, rides and dodgem cars – the first in the United Kingdom.

William Butlin was born in South Africa to British parents. Part of his childhood was spent in the company of his grandmother travelling around Britain with her family fair. After a few years in Canada and serving in the first World War, Butlin hired his own stall and trudged around the British Isles with his uncle's fair. By 1927 he had amassed enough money to put down roots and open his own static fairground on land leased from Major General Aldred Lumley, the 10th Earl of Scarborough.

His slides, stalls, rides and miniature railway were an instant success. The following summer Skegness saw the first dodgem cars to be imported into Britain. Always with an eye on raising capital for continued expansion, Butlin took the shrewd decision to buy exclusive European import rights for these fairground favourites. Visitors to his fairground already had his *Custer Cars* to ride on but these were battery powered cars to be driven in an orderly manner around a wooden track. Dodgems, or bumper cars, as they became known, gave the driver the opportunity to crash *"safely"* into other paying customers. With their overhead power supply and constant flashing of sparks, every fairground in the country had to have them.

Butlin knew that day-trippers could provide him with a steady income, but what he really needed was customers prepared to stay, and spend, for a week or more. Billy had observed, and experienced first-hand the ruthlessness of boarding house owners who would insist, often forcefully, on their occupants vacating the premises during the day, whatever the weather. Besides, guest houses and hotels were too expensive for most, especially in the years between the two world wars, so the canny entrepreneur set about expanding into the holiday accommodation market.

Ingoldmells lies about three miles north of Skegness and is reached by driving along the Roman Bank – a long straight road, whose name belies its origin. Butlin selected a flat site of former farmland sheltered by sand dunes but with ready access to a long stretch of clean sandy beach.

Famously, he drew the designs for his Skegness holiday camp on the backs of cigarette packets. Holidaymakers would rent a hundred square foot pastel-painted chalet erected at a cost of £10 each. Although each chalet was barely larger than a snooker table, Butlin wanted his visitors to feel at home, so flower beds and lawns were provided. Inside was pretty basic. You got somewhere to sleep, somewhere to sit, a cold-water supply, a single light and a mirror on the wall. No en-suite facilities or hot water! Each row of chalets shared a toilet block and bathing facilities. When you consider that Butlin's budget of £100,000 paid for 500 chalets, landscaping of a site that had previously been used to grow sugar beet, and a range of dining and entertainment services, you realise how good he was at squeezing the most out of his finances.

But, it was comfortable, homely and affordable for most. Prices started at 55 shillings a week (under £3), to include three meals a day and, as the newspaper advertisements stated *"Private bathing pool, boating lake, tennis courts, bowls, billiards, table tennis, all free"*. Little wonder, then that Butlin soon had to dip into his pocket to expand capacity. The first season sold out completely, with demand being so high that the Post Office requested Butlin arrange to pick up his own mail – so many booking requests were arriving every day. Within twelve months of opening, and after a further investment of £40,000, the site had expanded to hold 2,000 paying guests and now featured a gymnasium, theatre and fully-equipped dining room.

A couple of years later, the outbreak of World War II put a hold on developments in two ways. Firstly, holidays were the furthest things from the minds of most people but secondly, the War Office requisitioned the Skegness camp (and a second one at Clacton-on-Sea). The Ingoldmells site became HMS *Royal Arthur*, a "stone frigate" – as land based Royal Navy training establishments became known. Amongst those who served on-board were men and women learning specialist skills in wireless operations, codes and signals as well as members of the Royal Marines

Band. Being stationed on land wasn't always plain sailing! The Luftwaffe attempted to bomb the site several times – German radio even claimed to have "sunk" it on one occasion. Several men wrote later about poor living conditions. Descriptions of cold, draughty wooden chalets, whose only winter heating was one hot water pipe were common. The passing out song reflected the feelings of many:

"I had to join up, I had to join up,

I had to join old Butlin's Navy.

Ten bob a week, f*** all to eat,

Marching round the quarter deck with blisters on your feet,

I wouldn't give you tuppence for the whole damn lot!"

Given that the site was bombed over 50 times, including one attack in August 1940 that destroyed or badly damaged 900 chalets, it is remarkable that in the entire war, only one recruit lost his life aboard HMS Royal Arthur.

Billy Butlin received the site back from the Navy early in April 1946. By the 12th, he had placed advertisements in newspapers like the Lincolnshire Echo, recruiting "cooks, kitchen hands, waiters, waitresses, chalet-maids, cleaners and handymen" for the 1946 season. Within a month and a day, it was open for business once more.

At its peak, the site could accommodate close on 10,000 residential visitors as well as providing entertainment and catering facilities for several thousand more day-trippers. Butlin was a shrewd businessman, keeping one eye on press reviews and the other on the impact innovations by his competitors was having on revenue. Partly fuelled by some of the negative comments of servicemen and women stationed at HMS Royal Arthur and partly by the experiences of some customers, newspapers were often somewhat less than positive about the prospect of a family holiday at Butlin's. Billy's response was to create a more "up-market" feel to the site. A hotel was added just down the road from the main site, and alongside it a theatre. Both provided entertainment several nights a week and were open to the paying public as well as for residents of the holiday camp.

In 1948, Butlin opened his own aerodrome nearby. Charter flights would bring in holidaymakers and freight, and short sight-seeing flights could be bought (or won as prizes), offering visitors an experience they would not get if staying at one of Butlin's competitors. Following a trip to Disneyland in California, Billy invested £50,000 in the UK's first passenger monorail system.

Butlin's has continued to adapt to market changes. Now without the apostrophe and known as *Butlins Resort Skegness*, it continues to be important to the local economy, bringing in over a third of a million residential customers every year and providing employment to well over 1,000 local people.

One final thing we can thank Billy Butlin for. Ringo Starr was the drummer in the beat group *Rory Storm and the Hurricanes* in 1962. The band were midway through a summer season residency in Skegness when John Lennon and Paul McCartney drove from Liverpool to offer him Pete Best's position as full-time drummer in The Beatles. Starr was already known to McCartney and Lennon – he had stood in for Best before, so when the offer of a permanent position in the band, with a significant hike in pay, came along, Ringo didn't hesitate. In fact, he left Skegness more or less immediately.

As the concept of coastal resorts developed through the latter half of the nineteenth century and the early years of the twentieth century so more and more people moved to these areas seeking work. Many of them from overseas as we shall see next.

Further Reading:

A. Dowling, Humberston Fitties, Self-Published (2001)

W. Butlin & P. Dacre, The Sir Billy Butlin Story, Robson Books (1998)

I is for Ice-Creams and other Industries Immigrants have brought to the Lincolnshire Coast

You probably won't have heard of Augustine Fravigar, but if you have visited the east coast in the last hundred and fifty years, you will almost certainly have met one of his descendants. Augustine hailed from Genoa in Italy and was first recorded in Lincolnshire, lodging in a house in Boston in 1841. Forty years later the Fravigar family were establishing what would become an extremely successful business selling ice creams in Boston and Skegness from a portable cart.

Storing ice cream in the days before electric refrigeration was not easy. Ice cream was held in stainless steel tubs surrounded by ice and salt. The tubs had large metal lids and the whole cart was covered with a canvas or wooden canopy – often painted in bright colours to reflect the sun's rays. Even then, on hotter days, ice cream would melt in a few hours – thankfully trade on such days was generally better but it still meant regular runs back to the main storage facility to replenish supplies.

Another problem faced by competing traders was the often thorny issue of location. Things came to a head for the Fravigar business – by now trading in the name of Augustine Junior – in the summer of 1922. Selina, one of the daughters-in-law was in charge of the family ice cream barrow on the day in question. A popular spot to pitch the barrow was on the beach beside a long wind-break. Unfortunately, Alice Lawson had the same spot in mind for her cart. As the two ladies jostled for position, the whole thing got somewhat out of hand, leading ultimately to a court case a couple of weeks later. The *Skegness Standard* picked up the story under the headline:

RIVAL ICE-CREAM VENDORS AT VARIANCE

Mrs. Lawson testified under oath that *"it was the rule that those ice-cream vendors who got down to the beach first had the choice of pitches"*. Lawson claimed to have been there first, only for Mr. Fravigar to turn up and *"plant their stall a few feet away"*. Fortunately, Police Superintendent

Rawding of Spilsby happened to be on the beach at the time (eating, and enjoying, one of the Fravigar ice creams). He testified *"Mrs. Lawson struck Mrs. Fravigar and knocked her off the box, and when she got up struck her again."* After hair pulling, scratching and at least one kick, the policeman intervened, cautioning Mrs. Lawson and threatening to *"lock her up"*. You might think that the involvement of a senior police officer with over thirty years' experience could have a soporific effect, but no. The violent feud continued briefly, before sense finally prevailed. The outcome in court? Both women were bound over to keep the peace and fined £5 each.

The Fravigar family were well known throughout Boston and Skegness during the twentieth century. In addition to the ice cream business, Fred Fravigar had managed a haulage business shipping ice from the port of Boston, before taking on a confectionery business in 1924, selling rock and other sugary sweets on the seafront at Skegness. By 1950, Fred was running a factory manufacturing his own rock and a range of confectionery items including wine gums, toffee and fudge in the town. Sadly, the business was taken over in 2004 and the factory was closed down in 2013. Fred also owned a pleasure cruiser – The Royal Lady, a sixty-foot wooden motor boat, built in Grimsby in 1937. Other members of the family have operated fish and chip shops and restaurants, and the Fravigar name is still well known up and down the Lincolnshire coast. How many of those who are familiar with it realise the name originated with a Genoese travelling musician born almost two hundred years ago is anybody's guess.

Augustine Fravigar was just one of many Italians who brought the fashionable Mediterranean dessert to the United Kingdom, but ice cream is not an Italian invention. The concept of chilled fruit and ice based desserts almost certainly originated in China as much as 5000 years ago. Marco Polo, the Venetian merchant traveller and writer, most likely introduced them into Italy around 700 years ago, but it was not until the seventeenth century that ice creams in a form similar to those we consume today first appeared.

For a long time fishing has been a major industry along the Lincolnshire coastline, but the idea of frying fish, and ultimately, the seaside fish and chip shop has been traced back to Mediterranean countries. It is thought that migrant Spanish Jews in the seventeenth century were the first to fry fish in this country. The first fish and chip shop was opened in London in 1860, by Joseph Malin, another Jewish immigrant. Malin combined fish, coated in flour and fried, with chipped potatoes, previously only generally eaten by the Irish. The concept quickly spread to Lincolnshire, where fish and chip sellers soon sprang up close to the fish docks of Grimsby and Boston. Italian, Spanish and Portuguese migrants, already familiar with fish frying rapidly established successful businesses in these towns before expanding family operations inland and along the coast. Within 50 years, some estimate that England had as many as 10,000 fish and chip shops. By the 1930's local councils such as in the borough of Cleethorpes were passing special regulations permitting owners of Fish and Chip shops to open for business on Sundays.

At the end of 2016 new owners for Cleethorpes Pier were announced in the press. It seems that the *"Papa's Fish and Chip"* empire is expanding into their biggest operation yet – the UK's largest fish and chip restaurant with a dining capacity of at least 500! Dino Papadamou, one of the partners in the family business, in a recent interview with *Fry Magazine* recognised that his father Sid Papas built it from next to nothing. Sid *"a farmer's son"* first came to England in the 1960's *"with just £70 in his pocket"*. Sid got a job with an uncle in a fish and chip shop and after learning basic skills of filleting fish and preparing potatoes he soon had the urge to operate his own business, on the Kent coast at Margate. Time will tell what the impact will be on the many smaller independent fish and chip shops along the seafront, but for local residents, the prospect of 100+ new jobs in the town is welcome news.

Other *"traditional"* Lincolnshire seaside attractions include Punch and Judy (originated in Italy), deckchairs (first patented in the United States – but folding chairs were known in ancient Egypt), Miniature (or crazy) golf (known in China, the Netherlands, France and Scotland long before appearing in Lincolnshire), Frisbees (from the United States), Kites (China), slot machines (invented in San Francisco), Bingo (first known in Italy and then France, before arriving in England in its present form in the 1920's) and Candy Floss (invented in the United States), but fairground rides can be traced all the way back to thirteenth century England. Even sandcastles were known in the United States before reaching these shores.

Finally, a name you may not have heard of – John Carlbom. Although he may not be familiar to you, it is possible you have seen a statue donated by him in 1918 to the town of Cleethorpes – *The Boy With the Leaking Boot*? Carlbom, often misspelt as Calborn, was a Swedish national who lived and worked in the Grimsby area for much of his life, arriving in the county in the late 1880's. As well as establishing the shipping firm of Carlbom & Co. John served in the Swedish Consulate at Grimsby (one of several still existing in the port – including Denmark, Iceland and Norway). He had a strong affection for the area, and the country as a whole. Following his donation of three ambulances to the Port of Grimsby in 1917, the *Shields Daily News* explained Carlbom's generosity: *"it was up to every neutral who was enjoying the comfort and protection of this country to show his appreciation of that hospitality in such a way as he could"*.

Carlbom gifted many items to his adopted home over the years, including more than a hundred books to the library and a large trove of prehistoric, Roman, Saxon and Medieval antiquities donated to Lincoln Museum (on condition that once a suitable museum space became available in Grimsby, the collection would be rehoused – it is still in Lincoln, to this day). But what of the statue mentioned earlier? The original is displayed in the town hall with a replica standing in water in the Diana, Princess of Wales Memorial Garden. Unfortunately, it has become a regular target of vandalism in recent years, possibly because it symbolises immigration. There are dozens, possibly even hundred such statues around the world, yet its origin is unclear. Some argue that the boy represents an unfortunate young Italian newspaper vendor who drowned, but several other theories exist. The statue often appears around the world in major ports and centres of multicultural communities, but there is no evidence to suggest that Carlbom selected it for any other reason than that it had a *"twin"* in the land of his birth – Sweden.

So, our seaside towns and their customs owe much to the imports of goods, people and foreign cultural traditions – a point we would be wise to remember when we look next into the history of that most *"traditional"* English seaside town – Skegness.

Further Reading:

E. Gillett, A History of Grimsby, Hull University Press (1986)

L. Weiss, Ice Cream – A Global History, Reaktion (2011)

J is for a well-known Jolly Fisherman

When the Great Northern Railway (GNR) spent £12 on an illustration by John Hassall in 1908, no-one could have predicted that it would not only become the *"face"* of Skegness, but its impact would literally change the face of the emerging coastal resort. Hassall was employed as an advertising artist with the firm of David Allen & Sons and was already a prolific illustrator. His work commonly appeared in newspapers and on theatrical advertising posters and he went on to illustrate many children's books including Mother Goose's Nursery Rhymes in 1909. The artwork with its accompanying slogan "Skegness is SO bracing" first appeared over Easter in 1908 to promote special excursions from London at a cost of just three shillings return per passenger. The offer was so successful that it ran – at that price – for a full five years. By 1913 the annual total number of rail passengers arriving in Skegness had exceeded three quarters of a million and had virtually trebled since the introduction of Hassall's poster. In the 1914 summer peak eight-week season over 400,000 people flocked to Skegness aboard trains.

Hassall had never been to Skegness at the time of his commission, but he did visit the town in June 1936, where, in recognition of the effect his work had on the resort, he was honoured with *"the freedom of the foreshore"*. The artist enthused that Skegness had *"eclipsed all my anticipations"* adding *"it is even more bracing and attractive than I was led to expect"*. Twelve years earlier, the poster was almost scrapped. The London and North Eastern Railway Company, formed the previous year, and now encompassing GNR approached the Skegness Advancement Association requesting that the *"out of date"* poster and slogan be scrapped in favour of a new more modern campaign. The *Lincolnshire Echo* was able to report that Rev. William Disney rose to the challenge stating boldly *"the poster had proved to be the greatest friend the resort had ever possessed and he hoped the town would never consent to part with it"*.

Thankfully, the copyright to the artwork now belongs with the town itself – gifted by British Railways in 1966, along with Hassall's original artwork. This is now displayed within Skegness Town Hall on North Parade (closed at weekends). Should you arrive in Skegness by train, look out for a life-size statue of the Jolly Fisherman near the station entrance – you will see his rear first! The bronze statue has endured several trials of its own since originally being installed within the station concourse in 1989. In 2013 it required extensive and expensive renovation by the original sculptor Sioban Coppinger and in 2015 it survived a campaign by an animal rights group who wanted to replace the entire *"Jolly Fisherman"* mascot with an image of a dancing fish and a new slogan *"Skegness – A Happy Plaice"*. A second statue with a built-in water feature stands in Compass Gardens.

Prior to the rapid expansion of railway services in the nineteenth century, Skegness was a small fishing village and minor port. White's Directory of 1842 describes Skegness as *"a pleasant village and bathing place"* but also adds that it was *"until lately an obscure village"*. With a population of just 185 inhabitants the village was already embracing tourism by its *"several private lodging houses and two large and commodious hotels, which are provided with warm, cold and shower baths."* The two hotels were The Vine, and The New Hotel. As you might have realised, The Vine came first – but was originally known as The Skegness Hotel. By 1784, and known as The Vine, advertisements were being placed in London newspapers promoting Skegness as somewhere for those seeking sea bathing. However, the diarist John Byng on a visit to Skegness in 1791 was far from impressed, describing it as *"a vile, shabby bathing place"*. We can assume that Byng visited the Vine, since, at that time it was the only inn in the village. He clearly was not enamoured with the place *"There is no garden, no walk, no billiards room nor anything, for comfort or temptation. If a good house were built here, with a clever landlord, it would draw much company and answer well."* The Vine Hotel continues to this day, with a somewhat more favourable reputation. Sadly, Skegness's second hotel – The New Hotel, no longer exists. When Joseph Hildred took over the hotel on the corner of Lumley Road and High Street, he changed the name. Hildred's Hotel continued to operate in some shape or form until it was demolished in 1987. A shopping centre bearing the same name stands on the former hotel site.

The two Skegness hotels had become five by the end of the 1870's – The Lumley, The Ship and the Sea View all competing for the additional trade brought in on the new single-track railway line that had opened in 1873.

Hobson Dunkley and Charles Hildred, proprietors of the Sea View and Hildred's respectively represented traders associated with tourism on the board of a new private company – The Skegness Pier Co Ltd. The board's first action was to place advertisements in a host of newspapers announcing a competition to design *"the best … promenade pier"*. The winner would receive the contract to build it and a cash prize of £50 to boot. More than 40 entries were submitted and the winning plans came from the firm of Clarke and Pickwell in Hull. The Yorkshire engineers proposed to build a pier of just over 600 yards in length from cast iron to feature a 700-seater concert hall at its seaward end. Within a year, the foundation stone was laid and after a further eighteen months and £21,000 investment the pier was opened to the public.

Turnstiles at the entrance to the pier gave an instant opportunity to recoup some of that massive outlay. Even at just a penny admission charge, takings were impressive. On a single day in 1883 admission revenue was over £84. Within ten years of opening, annual turnstile revenue alone amounted to £400. One visitor from Leicestershire wrote on the subject of the pier in the *Skegness Herald* in July 1893:

"with its splendid promenade and cosy shelters terminating into a spacious 'head' and landing stage, the Pier presents many advantages to visitors in quest of recreation and rest."

The reviewer described the saloon areas daily entertainments as *"excellent"*, being *"of such a comprehensive character – ranging from the classical to the grotesque – that the most diversified tastes should be fully satisfied"*.

For those who wanted to venture out onto the sea itself, plenty of excursions by boat were available, not always without incident. In the same month as our Leicestershire reviewer visited Skegness, the *Lincolnshire Chronicle* published the following headline:

BOATING DISASTER AT SKEGNESS

---<>---

LOSS OF TWENTY-SEVEN LIVES

A large party of railway company employees, whilst enjoying a Saturday out at the seaside considered the possibility of enjoying a boat trip. Ultimately twenty-nine men from the party chartered a local boat – The *Shannon* – from Edward and Edwin Grunnill. Both were experienced sailors and members of the Skegness lifeboat crew. It had been a fine, warm summer morning, the boat would only be half full. What could possibly go wrong?

Weather can change suddenly at the best of times. At sea, this can have disastrous consequences. A great storm, whipped up by fierce winds forced all those ashore to seek shelter. Many of the railway company party made their way to the Pleasure Gardens where they had pre-arranged to dine in the Pavilion at 1pm. The *Shannon* had sailed *"some two miles from the pier head and about three quarters of a mile from the shore"* in the vicinity of the entrance to the Boston Deeps when a *"most unexpected squall"* caught the boat as it was turning to head back to shore so that "the doomed craft turned completely over". Another member of the Grunnill family, Jabez was out fishing at the time and managed to rescue three of the Londoners, but the rest drowned along with the two crewmen. Eleven railwaymen, along with fifteen of their friends and relatives left London that morning only to lose their lives on a day trip to the seaside. Hildred's Hotel served as a temporary morgue as bodies were recovered from the sea – some of them as much as three weeks later, others never recovered at all.

The Grunnill name continues to be associated with Skegness, the sea and lifeboats in particular. Joel Grunnill MBE, lifeboat chairman left a significant donation to the RNLI on his death in 2012. Following what the RNLI call a "significant donation" from his cousin April Grunnill, Skegness will be receiving a new *Shannon* Class lifeboat – The Joel and April Grunnill – early in 2017.

On that terrible day in 1893, the *Shannon* set sail directly from the beach, while steam boat trips ran from the pier. The Skegness Steamboat Company had been established shortly after the first steamer trips in 1882. A popular excursion involved a journey to Hunstanton in Norfolk, followed by a carriage ride inland to visit the Sandringham estate and then calling on the Lynwell lightship on the return journey. In July 1887, the *Skegness Herald* carried the following account from a passenger. Who after boarding the paddle steamer *Spindrift*:

"started from the Pier at 8.30 a.m. and arrived at the Norfolk coast about 11 a.m. A large number of the passengers utilised the opportunity to visit Sandringham, the charming residence of the Prince of Wales. A few went by train to Wolfreton, a mile-and-a-half from the Park, but most of the visitors went by road. The distance is eight miles, and an interesting and enjoyable drive; they formed themselves into parties of four or six, hired public conveyances and were driven there and hack for 2s. or 2s. 6d. each. The Spindrift paused as usual, both going and returning, at the Lynwell Lightship, which is six miles from Hunstanton and eleven from Skegness. There are always half-a-dozen men and an officer on duty, who frequently avail themselves of the visit of the Spindrift to post their letters, and for six weeks, they never leave their ship."

This particular twelve-hour excursion cost three shillings. For those with less money to spend, a one hour trip along the coast could be bought for a shilling. Bearing in mind that a weekly wage was often less than £1, one of these boat rides would have been a real treat.

Of course, the steamers also brought in day-trippers from Norfolk and further along the Lincolnshire coast – up to 7,000 a day arriving at the pier head. It was a relatively short-lived industry, however. As we have seen already, accretion along the coast line formed ever-larger sandbanks and created shallows near the pier head restricting access to the larger vessels. The prospect of entering a smaller boat and then transferring onto a steamer at sea was off-putting for many. Remember, these paddle steamers were mighty vessels. One of the first, The *May*, was 116 feet long and over 18 feet wide – imagine three double-decker buses in a line and you've just about got it. It was certified to carry over 250 passengers on the open seas.

Disaster struck the pier itself in March 1919. The Yorkshire Post reported the pier had been "CUT IN TWO". A Dutch vessel, The Europa, on its way from Amsterdam to Wisbech to collect a cargo of potatoes was caught out by what several newspapers reported as "cyclonic conditions" from the north-east. The ship, on her maiden voyage attempted to sit out the storm and dropped no fewer than four anchors (although some accounts claim only a single anchor was deployed). Matthew Grunnill, Coxswain of the Skegness Lifeboat called out his crew and horses, pulling the lifeboat to the water's edge in readiness for action. By now, the ship, with its motors halted was seen to be riding, apparently safely (for now) in just five feet of water. With the tide receding and the ship running aground, Grunnill spoke to the skipper, a man with the unfortunate name of Plougher, warning him that when the tide next came in, unless the storm abated, a collision with the pier was inevitable. Suffice to say, nature ran its course as expected and Plougher's *Europa* ploughed straight through the centre section of the pier before becoming lodged amongst a tangled mass of cast iron and timber. For Grunnill and his colleagues, the job of saving the eight crewmen involved negotiating the damaged pier and deploying ropes rather than using the lifeboat. The damaged cargo vessel was ultimately refloated and towed to Grimsby for £1000 worth of repairs. The pier lost an entire mid-section of almost 150 feet in length and cost over £3000 to rectify – more importantly, the job took twenty years to complete – just in time for the outbreak of the Second World War.

Fearing a land invasion, military strategists ordered the removal of the central section of the recently renovated pier (the North Sea had been generally known as the German Ocean prior to the previous World War). In a further attempt to prepare for all eventualities the Royal Navy were stationed at one end, the Air Force at the other with the Army keeping an eye on the middle. Perhaps no-one was ordered to keep an eye on the Pier itself, because by the end of the war it had fallen into such a state of disrepair that a further £23,500 had to be spent in repairs before it could once again open to the public in 1948.

Seaside holiday habits and preferences began to change significantly from the sixties onwards as families had more disposable income and the lure of foreign travels to tempt them away from a traditional trip to the British seaside. Skegness Pier underwent several re-inventions before finally nature determined its future.

In January 1978, a great storm, led to a tidal surge causing significant flooding and damage along the East coast. The pier at Skegness suffered minor flooding but more importantly, two sections of the pier itself were washed away, leaving the pier head and its 1000-seater capacity theatre cut off and open to the sea. Some pieces of Australian Jarrah wood were washed up over five miles away. Ever optimistic, owners submitted plans to link the landward and seaward sections with the world's first ever Pier monorail system, but funds never materialised and the theatre degenerated into a sanctuary for migrating birds until it was destroyed by a fire in 1985.

Now, all that remains amounts to 387 feet, just a fifth of the original pier and is home to a bowling alley, Laserquest and other amusements.

Tourism depends on visitors being able to get ready access to a resort. Most people nowadays tend to arrive in Skegness by road. East Lindsey District Council alone manage 10 car parks in Skegness. A 2011 survey concluded that the town had parking facilities for over 4,400 cars, more than double the provision of just 7 years earlier. In the same period, the number of cars on Britain's roads increased by over a million, and has risen by a million and a half since 2011, so we can assume that the demand for parking spaces is only going to go up further. This is all a far cry from the days of the first public car park in Skegness. In 1926, the district council opened a grassy field off the Grand Parade. There were no line markings or marshalling facilities resulting in chaotic scenes and several minor collisions before things took an organised turn for the better.

In those days, most visitors still arrived by rail, but there was an alternative form of wheeled transportation – the charabanc. This was the forerunner to the coach or minibus. Whether it was horse-drawn or motorised, it was characterised by having rows of seats (usually wooden - *char à bancs* is French for a carriage with wooden benches) facing forwards and was almost always open-topped. The Provincial Tramway Company was the leading provider of charabanc services bringing in parties of up to 40 at a time for day trips from the East Midlands, Lincolnshire and South Yorkshire.

But it was the railways that carried most visitors into Skegness – at its peak, up to sixty trains a day pulled into the station, packed with trippers. Prospective passengers could be forgiven if advertisements promoting the new service in 1873 led to amounts of confusion. Take this extract from the *Stamford Mercury* on 11th July:

GREAT NORTHERN RAILWAY

SATURDAY TO MONDAY OR TUESDAY

CHEAP EXCURSIONS

"Every Saturday (commencing 31st May ...) cheap tickets available ... From Nottingham ... to Skegness (it is expected that the Branch line to Skegness will be open early in June)".

Of course, this was the middle of July, and services did not actually commence until the 28th July. When they did, things got off to a rough start as the same newspaper reported the following month:

"as an excursion train from Gainsboro' and Lincoln was leaving (Skegness) ... the engine, on reaching the first points, ran off the rails, the wheels instantly being embedded in loose sand."

Being a single-track line, the subsequent delay impacted on passengers for the following trains well into the evening. This incident seemed not to deter future travellers – up to 700 passengers a day were purchasing tickets in the first month alone.

As we have seen, Skegness owes much of its shape and character to the designs of Henry Tippet and the drive and determination of the Earl of Scarborough, the area's major land owner in the nineteenth century. Tippet laid out the foreshore in a geometric grid, possibly inspired by Bristol, the town of his birth. Bristol was a bustling harbour, with access to the shore often complicated by a maze-like collection of narrow streets. Skegness had to be different. The largely affluent people seeking rest and recuperation amongst the fresh sea air needed light and space, so Tippet laid out homes in a series of broadly rectangular blocks, each with its own central courtyard, lined with trees and sheltered from the bracing north-easterly sea breezes of which Skegness was often prone.

Set amongst these were a market square and masonic hall as well as pleasure gardens, a pavilion, band stand and aquarium – all near to the "Grand Parade" – that most essential of Victorian seaside facilities – a promenade. Modern Skegness still features a promenade and pleasure gardens, but the seafront area is now largely a combination of car parks, diners and amusements. The village of under 200 people in the 1840's is now a town and permanent home to over 100 times as many residents as well as thousands more seasonal workers and holidaymakers. Skegness has something to suit most tastes, in spite of the assertion of Boris Johnson who wrote an article under a headline in the Daily Telegraph in 2008 *"Stuff Skegness, My Trunks and I are off to the Sun"*. Johnson was by no means the first person to write somewhat cruelly about the Lincolnshire Coast.

Further Reading:

A. E. Thompson, Skegness Pier 1881 – 1978, Self-published (1989)

A. J. Ludlam, Railways to Skegness, Oakwood Press (1997)

K is for Kali Kolsson's (not so) Kind words on the subject of Grimsby

The twelfth-century Norwegian Earl of Orkney, Rögnvald Kali Kolsson embarked on a pilgrimage to the Holy Land in 1151. In total, the Earl spent around two years away from Scotland. Somewhat earlier in his life, most likely as a teenager, he made a shorter pilgrimage – to Grimsby. His exploits are documented in five chapters of the Orkneyinga saga – a lengthy historical (and legendary) poetic history of the Orkney Islands.

It would seem from the poem that Kolsson spent some considerable time in Grimsby – but the impression it left on him might, on first consideration seem to be not particularly favourable. The poem states:

> *Vér hǫfum vaðnar leirur   vikur fimm megingrimmar;*
>
> *saurs vara vant, er várum,   viðr, í Grímsbœ miðjum.*

Which translates broadly into English as:

> *We waded in mire for five terrible weeks;*
>
> *There was no lack of mud where we were, in the middle of Grimsby.*

At the time, Grimsby was a very small settlement by modern standards. The Domesday Book records a population of just 32.5 households with 6 plough teams farming land only a few feet above sea level.

The geography of Grimsby has changed significantly since the days of Kolsson. Edward Gillett's excellent *History of Grimsby* describes the town as *"virtually an island with only one road into it at the end of the middle ages"*. Bearing this in mind, perhaps Kolsson was reflecting more on the difficult nature of the repeated journey between mooring place and the town, crossing mud-flats every time, than writing disparagingly about Grimsby itself. This theory is given additional weight when Ian Crockatt's careful translation of the same verse is used. In *Crimsoning the Eagle's Claw*, Crockett translates the same verse as:

Muck, Slime, Mud. We waded for five mired weeks, reeking, silt-fouled bilge-boards souring in Grimsby Bay.

Just how low the ground in the Grimsby area is can be illustrated by taking a look at Blundell Park, the home of Grimsby Town Football Club. Of all the 92 stadia in the English football leagues, Blundell Park is the lowest at just 2 feet above sea level. If we are nitpicking the stadium isn't strictly speaking in Grimsby – it is located on the Cleethorpes side of the A180 Grimsby to Cleethorpes road. The pitch itself is within 200 metres of the seafront.

Football can also help to illustrate industry in Grimsby at the beginning of the twentieth century. During this period, Grimsby Town and Hull City were given special dispensation (the only two clubs afforded the privilege) to play fixtures on Christmas Day. The official reason for this – demands of the local fish trade.

The fishing industry continues to this day, centred on what was once the largest working port in the world. Grimsby has been known as an important trading centre since at least the time of Kali Kolsson. The Orkneyinga saga records *Grimsboe* as being busy with a great number of traders from Norway, Scotland and the Suðreyjar (also known as *"the kingdom of the isles"* and consisting of The Hebrides, the Firth of Clyde islands and the Isle of Man). Even before that, there is some archaeological evidence of a small Roman presence in the Grimsby area. Opinions are divided as to the motivation behind Roman developments in the area. Certainly, it afforded a relatively safe, sheltered harbour and was a good place to land fish in large stocks, but the nearest large settlement at *Lindum* (Lincoln) was over 40 miles away. Furthermore, a quarter of the journey would have required travel across country or along dirt tracks.

No, I believe the Romans occupied land around Grimsby so that they could work the plentiful supplies of chalk nearby. The Celtic word *Cleis* from which some scholars argue that Cleethorpes derives its modern name, in fact, means chalk. The Romans needed chalk as aggregate for their roads, to mix with clay in order to make vast quantities of cement for their baths and aqueducts. It was even used in cosmetics and in coffins to preserve bodies.

What cannot be disputed is that the Romans installed a long unbroken line of signal stations along the East Coast of England. Holm (sometimes spelled with a terminal 'e') Hill is one of several man-made mounds in and around Grimsby believed to have once been the site of a Roman signal station. Unsurprisingly, since much of the *"hill"*, like the other six nearby, has been either eroded or quarried, little evidence other than the name itself still exists.

This last piece of evidence helps to establish Grimsby as one of the world's major settlements built on or around seven hills – up there with Jerusalem, Athens, Rome, Mecca and San Francisco! It's just a bit smaller, and always has been. Take the beginning of the nineteenth century as an example. Grimsby had a population of around 1500, Jerusalem around 8,000, Athens around 4,000, Mecca was estimated at 30,000 – 40,000 and Rome muscles into our list at around 150,000. What about San Francisco you ask? Back then it was only half the size of Grimsby, but now has 10 residents for every Grimbarian, as the folk of Grimsby are sometimes known.

Grimsby doesn't appear to hold a grudge against the Norwegian nation or its people for the writings of Kali Kolsson. In fact, the town is twinned with Tromsø, a northern Norwegian city of a similar size and hosts an honorary consulate at Sutcliffe House, in Flour Square. The concept of twinning emerged after World War II in an attempt to spread international harmony, cooperation and trade. In recent years many places have "adopted" more than one twin, and sometimes for more, shall we say, novelty reasons. Hence the twinning of the Scottish town of Dull with Boring in Oregon and Bland in Australia, for example.

Modern-day Grimsby struggles to cope with the demands of twenty-first century social and economic life. Critics point to the loss of port trade, a decline in moral values and the rise of competition for business elsewhere – most notably the city of Hull on the other side of the Humber. One observer wrote very clearly on this subject, citing three reasons for the *"decay"* of what he affectionately referred to as a *"very great and rich"* town:

"First, the destruction of the haven (as a result of silt deposits from erosion at nearby Cleethorpes). The second was the destruction of the religious

houses there. The third ... was the rise of Hull, which ... robbed them (Grimsby) ... (not only) of all their traffic, but also of their chief tradesmen."

Who wrote these words? Abraham De La Pryme. When? 1697.

Before we move on, I think it is worth offering a small crumb of comfort for those of you are still feeling upset by Kolsson's description of Grimsby. What Daniel Defoe had to say about Lincoln in 1724 was far worse. In his *Tour Through the Whole Island of Great Britain* he recorded that the city was *"ancient, ragged, decay'd, and still decaying ... full of the ruins of monasteries and religious houses"*. Since Lincoln is not, and never has been, on the coast, we will leave it at that. Our look at Kolsson took us back to the twelfth century. Our next story is set in the thirteenth. Have you ever lost something like a key or a banknote that had perhaps been in a trouser pocket before your clothing went in the laundry? Read on for a story of something rather more valuable being lost in the wash!

Further Reading:

P. Chapman, Grimsby: The Story of the World's Greatest Fishing Port, DB Publishing (2014)

More on Kali Kolsson at:
http://skaldic.abdn.ac.uk/db.php?table=verses&id=3637&val=interact

L is for the Loss of King John's Jewels

If you study the outline of the British Isles, paying attention to the many estuaries, one will probably stand out from the rest. The Thames, The Humber, The Severn along with most of the others are all jagged, almost sharks tooth in shape. There is, however, a single "estuary" shaped very much like a human molar tooth. Straddling the border between Lincolnshire and Norfolk, The Wash is in fact the estuary for no less than four rivers – The Great Ouse, The Witham, The Nene and Welland rivers all find their way to the sea here. Studies have shown these four rivers once merged and fed into the sea as a single body of water.

So, how did The Wash get its distinctive shape? Ice! But not as you might expect from the glaciated river channel pushing down to the sea. In their 1998 book *Glaciers and Glaciation*, Douglas Benn and David Evans identified a long deep valley in the North Sea bed about 15 miles east of the Spurn peninsula running for close to 30 miles in the direction of The Wash. The *Silver Pit* as it became known, has steep canyon walls dropping almost 100 metres below the sea floor in places and was the product of a much older advancement of ice from the north. Glaciers tend to carve out u-shaped channels as opposed to the v-shaped valleys formed by free-flowing water. The Wash with its idiosyncratic 200+ square mile square "*bay*" being the result.

At this point you may be wondering about the use of punctuation around the words "*estuary*" and "*bay*" earlier, so let's clear this up. Strictly speaking, The Wash is not an estuary at all, but a large bay with four distinct estuaries flowing into it.

The area of low-lying land around The Wash is very fertile, prime agricultural land. Evidence of its use for farming dates to at least Roman times. Being low-lying, flooding is always a problem – even though, the receding flood waters leave behind mineral-rich silt deposits. As a result, flood defences and land reclamation works punctuate the coastline, particularly along the Lincolnshire boundaries of The Wash.

Surveys have revealed this unique feature of our coastline is shrinking at quite an alarming rate. Centuries of accretion has led to many coastal towns and villages steadily creeping inland as we saw in our first chapter. Recent studies carried out on behalf of Ordnance Survey have shown that over 5 square miles of The Wash have been claimed back from the sea in the last forty years or so. A study of saltmarshes showed a general increase in size of around 30% between 1992 and 2006. Eventually it is likely that The Wash as we know it will disappear from our coastline completely.

Talking of disappearing, the point of this chapter is to tell the story of how King John came to lose the Crown Jewels so let us begin with the legend. The tale is a pretty simple one. The King had been staying in the Lincolnshire town of Spalding and had departed on a journey to Bishop's Lynn in Norfolk. (King's Lynn was formerly known as Bishop's Lynn until King Henry VIII took control of the town from the Bishop of Norfolk in 1537). Apparently, feeling unwell, John ordered his driver to turn around and head for Swineshead Abbey, taking a slow but safe route via Wisbech. His baggage train of several carriages carrying a substantial weight in clothing and regal possessions including the Crown Jewels was instructed to take a more direct but risky route along the causeway in the area between what are now Long Sutton and Sutton Bridge (remember at this time, these were coastal settlements and so the route would only have been passable at low tide).

You can guess the rest! The tide came in and caught the convoy unawares and unable to escape the advancing waters. Legend has it that much of the baggage train succumbed to the sea and the Crown Jewels were lost forever. Several attempts have been made to study the area and establish a possible location for the bootie. Some put it at Fosdyke in the estuary of the River Welland, others reckon the treasure site to be further to the west. The one thing that is pretty much guaranteed is that after 800 years of accretion and agriculture, anything buried will be so well covered as to be virtually impossible to locate.

But there are further twists to this tale. Firstly, the baggage train would have been accompanied by several hundred men, many of them experienced soldiers and the Kings most trusted advisors and supporters. Is it conceivable that all of them lost their lives? That not a single account from a survivor exists? Some believe that the Crown Jewels were not lost at all but were smuggled away on the King's orders to conceal his possessions from any possible future claimants.

The second, perhaps even more controversial possibility is that King John's illness was caused by a deliberate act. Reports suggest that John was suffering from dysentery, which some have suggested may have been a consequence of poisoning. He never recovered from this illness and died a few days later in Newark. He was just 49 years old. John had a personality described by one biographer as "distasteful" and was prone to acts of "pettiness, spitefulness and cruelty" so had built up a long list of enemies and capable suspects even amongst his own ranks.

What do we know for certain? Only that the King's jewels were lost a few days before the King himself and that no trace of them has been seen to this day.

The Wash does have plenty of its own treasures that can be viewed freely. Unsurprisingly, given that it is home to the largest nature reserve in the United Kingdom. Here you can find the biggest colony of common seals in England as well as flocks of geese, waders and other seabirds. Don't forget to keep a look out for predators such as marsh harriers stalking prey above the saltmarshes and mudflats.

A word of caution. Marshes and wetlands can be very dangerous places. Plan your visit carefully. Stick to waymarked routes and do not be tempted to stray from footpaths. If venturing near the sea pay careful attention to tide times and local information boards – stay safe at all times, you are more precious than any crown jewels!

Before we leave King John behind, it should be mentioned that the "Port" of Boston was granted a Royal Charter by the King in 1204, entitling the town to host international trade fairs. These were huge events over several days, raising so much revenue for the crown by way of taxation, that Boston was the second largest contributor behind London.

The Port of Grimsby was granted its own Royal Charter by the same King three years earlier. The charter granted local administrative powers to the people of the town, but more importantly to the King it enabled him to have more effective taxation regimes in place to exploit the ever-increasing flow of goods arriving in Grimsby. At this time, Scandinavian timber, French and Spanish Wine and, of course, Fish were all regular arrivals. John himself only went to Grimsby once, and then in anger, in 2016, shortly before losing the Crown Jewels.

The "Wash" legend may or may not be based on fact – elements of it are quite corny. The next chapter is totally based on fact – and is very corny.

Further Reading:

R. Waters, The Lost Treasure of King John, Tuccan Books (2014)

H. Irving, Tidal Havens of the Wash and Humber, Imray (2011)

M is for Millers and their Mills

Lincolnshire still has well over 100 windmills standing – some of them operational, others converted into living accommodation and a few just a shell to remind of a once thriving industry. Thirty or so of them are on or close to the coast but if you ask anyone to show you a windmill, they will almost certainly point an arm out to sea where an ever-increasing number of wind turbines turn almost incessantly, generating electricity for much of the East coast.

So, before we look into the traditional art (more of a science really) of harnessing wind power, perhaps the modern incarnation is worth closer examination. The Lincs Wind Farm is five miles off the coast of Skegness and comprises 75 turbines spread over an area of 13 square miles. Each 330 feet high steel cylinder houses a set of rotors with a diameter approaching 200 feet. The turbines are spaced almost a third of a mile apart and stand in nearly 50 feet of water. Between them is a total generating capacity of 250 megawatts. This is enough to boil around 10 million kettles simultaneously, or provide electrical power for a town the size of Grimsby. All this comes at a price – the project cost in excess of £1 billion, and the farm has an expected operational life of no more than 40 years. Alongside Lincs are the older twins – Lynn and Inner Dowsing in the shallows at the entrance to The Wash. These have been operating in tandem since 2009 and generate up to 20 megawatts from their 54 turbines.

Offshore wind farms attract plenty of criticism. Concerns abound – they are thought to be noisy, they may cause increased water pollution due to increased traffic flow, they may affect habitat, even that they may be a dangerous obstacle for shipping. Yet, there may well be significant environmental benefits. The seabed foundations can act as artificial reefs increasing shellfish stocks and, as a consequence, other marine life within the shellfish food chain. The farms may deter shipping and therefore create a calm buffer zone that attracts fish and thereby increases stocks. There is no doubt that using renewable energy sources like wind is infinitely better for the atmosphere than continuing to burn fossil fuels.

One of the oldest windmills along the Lincolnshire Coast is at Saltfleet. Built around 1770, originally from timber like most early mills, it was substantially altered to a brick structure at the end of the nineteenth century. Saltfleet's mill like most in the region, was used to grind corn. With a traditional onion cap (or ogee), the mill was in regular use until the 1950's after which, despite becoming a listed building, it fell into disrepair for some time. Now restored and featuring a large building added to the side, it is a rather attractive residential property, with one of the mills own stones standing beside the entrance. The mill can be found beside the A1031 coast road in the village.

At nearby Alford, a fine example of a five-sailed windmill not only survives to this day, but is in full operational use AND open to the public. At the peak of corn production in the county, Alford had four mills, all built by local millwright, John Oxley. This one dates to 1837. Oxley passed away in September 1850 at the age of 49, having fallen from another mill three months earlier whilst painting one of the sails, at Barrow, North Lincolnshire. Some works give the name of "Sam" Oxley as the millwright, including the windmill's own website, but the entry in White's Directory for Alford in 1842 only lists "John" as millwright for the village. The 1841 census would also suggest that it was John and not Sam that was responsible for this fine construction.

The Alford mill design was heavily influenced by the writings of the famous engineer, John Smeaton. In a paper published in 1759 "*An Experimental Enquiry Concerning the Natural Powers of Water and Wind to Turn Mills and Other Machines Depending on Circular Motion*", Smeaton passed on to millwrights around Britain models for designing efficient mills, giving contemplation to the optimum number of sails, their lengths, angles of rotation, even the most efficient cloth design was considered. Smeaton is also widely credited with being the first western engineer to recognise and use the aerodynamic properties of the ogee in mill design.

Oxley and others built several different mills in Alford. The surviving mill has five sails, but others in the village had four, even one with six. Myer's Mill was most unusual, featuring not only six wooden sails, but angled "left-handed" it was aligned the opposite way round to almost all other Lincolnshire mills.

When milling and storing corn and other grains, the building has to remain dry at all times. Should you visit the Alford mill you will notice that it has a blackened exterior. This is a layer of tar covering the brickwork to insulate the mill and its precious contents from damp. With a gleaming white onion cap and sails in full flow, the mill is a most impressive sight.

Visitors can see the mill in full operational condition (If there is no wind, an engine takes over!) and can purchase a wide variety of milled products as well as touring six of the seven floors and walking around the third-floor exterior gallery.

Why did Alford warrant four corn mills in such a small area? Perhaps the answer lies in the canal that was never dug. Between 1765 and 1825 no fewer than five reports and estimates were commissioned into the feasibility of building a canal connecting the village with the coast, five miles away. Corn was being grown at a plentiful rate, there was a large demand for milled corn flour throughout western Europe. In 1826, the proposals gained royal assent as *"An Act for making and constructing a Canal, from the town of Alford, in the county of Lincoln, to the Sea, at or near the village of Anderby, in the said county, with a Basin, Harbour, and Pier"*. The plan was costed at £38,000 of which £30,000 had already been raised. The only problem was that no-one was prepared to finance the balance and the project which would have considerably sped up the process of packing and transporting corn products overseas was never materialised.

We began this section by looking out to sea at "windmills" that aren't really mills at all. However, some mills do utilise water and Lincolnshire had a very fine example of one, at Claythorpe, a further 5 miles inland from Alford. Some might consider this to be too far inland to be included in a book about the coast, but it can be reached in around a quarter of an hour from Mablethorpe. The watermill has not been used for several decades but visitors can still view a selection of cogs and millstones, whilst dining in a café overlooking the site of the original mill wheel. A fire in 1889 destroyed much of the building and the water wheel. When the owner, J.W. Chambers rebuilt the following year, he modernised the facility by replacing the wheel with a steam turbine. Nowadays, the site is a popular tourist attraction featuring extensive wildfowl gardens and is home to otters, wallabies and marmosets as well as several other species of animals.

Windmills continue to fascinate people of all ages and the Lincolnshire coast has the remains (restored/revised or otherwise) of several that can be seen close at hand at Addlethorpe, Barrow and Burgh le Marsh amongst others. Some are no more than stumps, converted into living accommodation, such as the one at Trusthorpe, while others have been restored and are in full operational order – one of the best of these is the magnificent Maud Foster Windmill on the Northern fringes of Boston. The 80-foot tall, five-sailed mill stands beside a deep drain cut around 1568 that also bears the name of the same lady. The identity of Maud Foster has never been revealed, other than that she appears on several documents in the sixteenth century that lead me to infer she must have been a very wealthy lady, and therefore, most likely a widow who inherited her fortune as a result of being childless. The windmill itself celebrates its bicentenary in 2019. Be aware if you plan to visit that opening is restricted and that, like all mills, if you want to see it operating, its best to wait for a windy day!

Before we leave, there is a final milling-related story from the Alford area, but a gruesome one. It concerns the 1823 murder of a woman by the name of Sarah Arrowsmith. The woman had been in an extended relationship with a local man called John Smith, in fact having born a son by him and also carrying a second child at the time of her death. Smith's motives remain unclear to this day, but the evidence presented at his trial was crystal clear. He purchased a large quantity of arsenic, mixed it in with a sack of flour and persuaded Sarah to use it. The unsuspecting woman baked a batch of oatcakes and rapidly became violently ill. In spite of medical intervention neither her life or that of her unborn child could be saved. Smith was tried and found guilty of murder at Lincoln Chapter house the following March. The judge Baron Hullock, sentenced Smith to be hanged, dissected and anatomised. For several years afterwards the murderers severed hand was displayed in the village apparently.

A severed arm of a different kind was behind an unsolved mystery in January, 2009. Many local residents reported seeing bright flashing lights in the night sky off the Lincolnshire night-time coast. The following morning, one of the wind turbines was spotted to have two badly mangled arms, and a third missing completely. The conclusion of many was that a low-flying alien spacecraft had crashed into the turbine in the dark. Others suggested that the Royal Air Force were conducting secret test flights off Donna Nook and that one mission had finished with an accidental collision. We will probably never know what really happened.

Happily, though, there is plenty that can be told about Donna Nook.

Further Reading:

J. Sass, Windmills of Lincolnshire, Stenlake Publishing (2012)

To keep up to date with offshore wind farm developments visit:

http://www.4coffshore.com/windfarms/lincs-united-kingdom-uk13.html

N is for Nook

One dictionary defines a nook as a corner or recess, particularly offering seclusion or security. The *"Nook"* we are interested in here – *Donna Nook* might not feel particularly secure when it is being used by the Royal Air Force for bombing practice but it is sufficiently secluded to attract a very large colony of grey seals who return to breed along this short stretch of Lincolnshire's coastline annually towards the end of each year.

Almost halfway between Cleethorpes and Mablethorpe the coastline takes a short but very distinct turn to the south. This corner is the *"Nook"*. So, who is *"Donna"*? Legend has it that *The Donna* was a ship – part of the Spanish Armada fleet, wrecked just off the coast here in 1588. Unfortunately, it's not that simple. The armada did lose some ships off the east coast, but not one by the name of Donna. Others have proposed the name was that of a woman whose body was washed up on the shore, but again without proof. All that is certain is that our secluded bomb site cum seal sanctuary has gone by that name for at least 250 years.

The grey seal population varies from year to year but in a typical autumn around two thousand pups are born here within a matter of a few weeks. Understandably this event is very popular with visitors and attracts thousands into the area every year. Donna Nook Nature Reserve is in the care of the Lincolnshire Wildlife Trust who manage the site and pay particular attention to the welfare of the large grey seal colony. For much of the year these surprisingly large mammals (bulls can reach 10 feet in length and weigh up to 680 pounds – about the same as a motorbike and sidecar, with rider and child passenger!) are out at sea or basking on the distant offshore sandbanks, but towards the end of October they seek out the beaches at the foot of the dunes and prepare to expand their families.

Grey seals have a voracious appetite, needing around 11 pounds of fresh food every day. They have been observed diving to depths of around 250 feet to hunt and will eat most varieties of fish as well as octopus. These are mean predators and have been seen taking on harbour porpoises as well as other seals. Seal pups can weigh in at 30 pounds or more at birth and will feed solely on their mother's ultra-high fat milk for the first month of their lives, before swimming out to sea in search of their own food.

At the nature reserve, priority rightly is given to the welfare of the seals, so expect to find plenty of fencing and warning signs. Please observe all the instructions diligently – seal pups are easily frightened and, once startled and separated from their mothers they may not find them again and can starve to death. The other reason for extra care is that seal calves are very protective towards their offspring and will attack any perceived threat – even a human one. Seals have a very nasty bite, and although injuries from grey seals are rare, it is best to keep a safe distance. That said, even behind the fences, you may well find yourself within a handful of feet of several seals and their somewhat cute and fluffy pups.

Should you visit, please remember that car parking and toilet facilities are limited – check the nature reserves website for details. Also, before taking photographs, be sure to read the photographers code of conduct on the same website.

In November 2011, storm surges caused several of the seal pups to become detached from their mothers, with tragic consequences. As many as 75 pups are believed to have died. A similar tidal surge two years later led to the destruction of much of the spectator fencing and nearby information huts. In spite of the efforts of many reserve wardens, large numbers of seals were washed inland by the exceptionally high tide. Although most were successfully located and assisted back to the shore, one unfortunate grey seal died after being struck by a car. Three other seals were rescued, having become trapped in a ditch three miles from the sea. The scale of destruction, to both the colony and the reserve itself, led to the wildlife trust closing the site for the remainder of the 2013 season.

Destruction of one area of the site is a regular and deliberate event. The Royal Air Force have maintained a presence at Donna Nook since 1927, when it was first used as a bombing range. A seven mile stretch of coastline was marked and equipped with five large observation towers so that bombing raids could be monitored and assessed. Flight crews were allocated targets up to 8,000 yards out at sea, with bombs released from altitudes of up to 14,000 feet. Nine years later, an airfield was established as a relief landing site with plans to lay permanent runways so that the station could become home to a squadron of bombers, but the onset of World War II forced a rethink. Until the summer of 1941, RAF Donna Nook was no more than a decoy site with rows of wooden and fabric mock-ups of twin-engined Bristol Blenheim light bombers standing out in the open, hoping for the Luftwaffe to be tricked into wasting their arms on these decoys. The deception worked on more than one occasion.

Nearby RAF North Coates was struggling to cope with Coastal Commands requirements, so the airfield at Donna Nook was requisitioned as a reserve strip. For around a year or so, 206 Squadron based its Lockheed Hudson bombers at the airfield. Very little evidence remains that this was one of the sites from which the so-called *"thousand force"* targeted the German city of Bremen in Operation Millennium II during June 1942. Several air force men died in that mission as well as more than 80 German civilians, but the greatest loss of military life occurred earlier in the year when one of five Hudson bombers, part of 407 squadron of the Royal Canadian Air Force, crashed into the air traffic control tower while attempting to return from a sea strike mission. The bomber still had its complement of arms on board and exploded on impact, killing all four of its flight crew as well as 13 members of ground staff in the vicinity at the time.

For the final years of the war, RAF Donna Nook was home to a CHEL (Chain Home Extremely Low) RADAR station, where a young Arthur C Clarke was stationed and in fact, gained his pilot's licence. It was at this time Clarke also began regularly publishing science fiction stories in fanzines. CHEL RADAR was very important as it could detect very low flying aircraft that conventional RADAR systems missed. It could even pick up German *Schnellboots* or E-Boats as these super-agile motor torpedo boats of the Kriegsmarine were known in Britain.

Facilities at North Coates had been upgraded, with the provision of longer concrete runways so eventually, RAF Donna Nook became redundant for flying purposes. From 1944 onwards the site was transformed into a Prisoner of War camp where it became home for around 3,000 mostly Polish and Ukrainian members of the German army, captured in France.

Many of them chose to remain in Lincolnshire after the war rather than return to their homelands under communist control.

The great floods of 1953, mentioned elsewhere in this book, washed away most of the structural evidence of the site so that modern aerial photography reveals little evidence of the RAF stations existence prior to life as a bombing range. These have always been dangerous shores. Dozens of ships have been wrecked off the coast of Donna Nook over the years. In 1835 a beacon was erected on the shoreline. Trinity House announced the initiative in newspapers including the *Hull Packet* with a style typical of the period:

NOTICE TO MARINERS

TRINITY-HOUSE, HULL

15th October, 1835

NOTICE is hereby given, that this Corporation have ERECTED a BEACON upon the Low Sandy Point of the LINCOLNSHIRE SHORE commonly called DONNA NOOK on the South side of the entrance into the River Humber as a distinguishing Sea Mark for the guidance of Ships and Vessels entering the said river from the Southward.

The wooden tower, known locally as "Gazzy Buoy", was 50 feet high, pyramid-shaped and painted red with a conical cap and gave shipping a valuable reference point with visibility of up to 14 miles in clear conditions – extremely important protection from the dangerous sandbanks lying offshore. Twelve years later, the beacon was declared to be the southernmost point of a zone stretching northwards beyond Spurn Point to Dimlington (a mile north of Easington, and since lost to coastal erosion) which would fall under the jurisdiction of specially appointed "Humber Pilots" – locally experienced master mariners who would safely steer all shipping in and out of the ports of Hull, Goole and Grimsby.

In 1858 plans were submitted for a permanent coastguard Station adjacent to the beacon (A lifeboat had been based here with quite basic facilities since 1829). This was built and opened the following year. Nowadays the name Donna Nook is still associated with a coastguard service, but the modern station is actually in nearby North Somercotes.

The importance of coastguards – a volunteer service, funded largely by charitable donations cannot be overstated. When the Lincolnshire coast increased its lifeboat provision in 1870, the *Lincolnshire Chronicle* reported that the Donna Nook boat had already been responsible for saving 110 lives. Sadly, the outcome is not always positive. In April 1966, the Scottish twin-engined passenger vessel, Anzio I on a voyage from Tilbury to Scotland in weather described by the official inquest as a *"northeasterly gale, with squalls of sleet and rain and varying visibility"* became stranded off Donna Nook late at night. The ship was so close to shore that a member of the Donn Nook coastguard was able to wade towards her and hail the crew members on board, but he could not be heard and the ship was listing badly. When a large wave took the coastguard off his feet, he returned, exhausted and in an anxious state to the nearby coastguard station. Within four hours and despite repeated efforts to save the crew, the Anzio I was completely submerged and the lives of all thirteen hands on board had been lost.

So, if, and when you visit the nature reserve and marvel at the wonders of the grey seals, caste your eyes out to sea and spare a thought for the dozens of mariners who met their deaths in the same waters that spawn so much new life every year.

The Lincolnshire Coast has a very new facility from which the sea can be viewed – more on this coming up next.

Further Reading:

M. Osborne, 20th Century Defences in Britain: Lincolnshire, Brassey's (1997)

For updates on the seal colony at Donna Nook visit:

http://www.lincstrust.org.uk/donna-nook/weekly-update

O is for Observatory

As you have read through this book you will have probably noticed that most sections are concerned with how things are and/or how they once were. This chapter is different in that much of it relates to something that has yet to be completed (at the time of writing – early 2017). But first, a little bit of history.

One website describes Chapel St. Leonards as a place *"where the country meets the sea"*. In February 1953, the sea met the country with lethal consequences. The *Lincolnshire Standard and Boston Guardian* printed a photo of a *"brick-built bungalow … cut almost in half"* above a shocking headline announcing the deaths of 10 residents. Such was the force of the North Sea Flood (or *Watersnoodramp* as it was known elsewhere – much more of this later). The same newspaper established that 14 houses had been completely demolished as *"the seas lashed over the sandhills breaking the sea defences"*. These had only been completed the previous year. Snack bars disappeared and a car was washed several hundred yards inland by the ferocious waves. The entire village of Chapel St. Leonards remained flooded for several days.

This was not the first flood to decimate "Chapel". Back in the sixteenth century the village of Mumby Chapel – a full mile inland – was engulfed by an enormous tide, destroying the medieval church and much of the village. Over time, Mumby and Chapel developed close ties, becoming known collectively as Mumby-cum-Chapel for a long period. At the time of the 1841 census Mumby-cum-Chapel was actually twice the size of its southerly neighbour, Skegness. In 1895, the parishes of Mumby and Chapel officially separated, and Chapel St. Leonards came into existence in its own right. Of course, Chapel St. Leonards was already a popular seaside destination. The Vine Hotel (not the 1930's reincarnation) offered visitors a *"house … replete with every accommodation for Public and Private Families"* (*Stamford Mercury* – 1879). The same newspaper also advertised the sale of newly built holiday homes as follows:

> *"The houses which were built for the reception of seaside visitors, are*
> *fitted with every convenience, and, from the superior accommodation*

which they afford, always command the best class of tenants. There is an excellent sea view from the front windows and from a projecting balcony extending the whole length of the building."

Prospective investors were assured that for *"an active and energetic Lodging-housekeeper the speculation would prove very remunerative."* Nowadays the village still has its fair share of boarding houses, but is probably best known for a multitude of sprawling holiday parks (or caravan sites, depending on your preference). The majority of Chapel's four and a half thousand permanent residents are over the age of 55 and getting older, so facilities in the village tend to cater for the more mature and sedate older population as well as the more energetic, and often younger holidaymakers whose numbers swell the population four-or even five-fold in the summer months.

One new arrival at Chapel promises to attract all ages. This is the North Sea Observatory. Lincolnshire County Council describe the structure as *iconic* and promise that it will offer *"fantastic, uninterrupted views of dunes, beach and North Sea"* from its location at Chapel Point. To be fair, some will look at the design, featuring seven massive triangular sea-facing windows and suggest that it offers no better views than can be afforded by standing on the beach, and this is true, but the building will attract visitors who might not otherwise come to the area, will provide up to 50 jobs for local people and has given valuable work to those employed in construction at a time when work is hard to come by. The project has taken a long time to become a reality, with massive hurdles to overcome along the way. Originally envisaged to be located at Huttoft Bank near Sandilands, the position was moved to Chapel Point in 2013 following concerns raised by residents about increased traffic flow to the area. It seemed that all were in agreement that a coastal country park stretching along the five miles from Sandilands to Chapel St. Leonards was an excellent proposition but that Chapel Point offered the best site for the observatory itself.

A change in location required a change in design. The original plans featured a somewhat jagged, pointed structure, raised above the beach to allow for the natural movement of sand underneath the structure to continue. The Chapel Point design is very different in shape, some say it bears more than a passing resemblance to the lower half of a clam shell but retains the mandatory requirement from the original tender to be "raised above the sand dune to minimise the impact on both the existing sea defences and the archaeology".

Once the location had been finalised and funding secured, the £1.75 million project could get underway. Unfortunately, early excavations of the site unearthed Second World War smoke bombs as well as long-forgotten sea defences covered over since the 1953 storms. As a result, laying of foundations was massively delayed so that the structure is not scheduled to be complete and open to the public before the summer of 2017.

When completed the observatory will have much to live up to. Lincolnshire County Council describe it as *unique* and specified in the original tender that it must *"have several uses, primarily as an Observatory for watching the migrating sea birds with factual nature displays, but it will also incorporate a small art gallery/activities area and a Café."* The tender went on to state that *"Both the Café and Art Gallery will also have areas of external decking for seating and displays respectively"* as well as *"provision for the Costal (sic) Watch volunteer service that assist the coast guards in identifying any problems at sea."*

So, when you visit the Observatory, what can you expect to observe? If you are already a birdwatcher you will know that many different species of birds follow the Lincolnshire Coastline as part of their annual migratory routes every spring, autumn or winter. As many as a million birds pass by every year, including flocks of Mediterranean gulls, godwits, puffins, geese, snipes, swans and warblers. If birdwatching is new to you, don't worry, part of the thinking behind the observatory is that it will attract people like you and there will be information boards and people to answer any questions you might have. Should your eyes be more attracted to the water than the skies, look out for harbour porpoises, dolphins, seals and whales – all are regular visitors.

During World War II, people looked to the skies beyond Chapel Point with an air of dread rather than excited expectation. Some had seen German Zeppelins fly over in the First World War. In April 1916, one dropped three bombs on nearby Alford after crossing the coastline at Chapel. Twenty years later, perhaps the most well-known airship of them all, Hindenburg, passed over Chapel St. Leonards on its return flight to Germany from the United States. The *Skegness News* carried the observations of a Hogsthorpe man who stated:

"it flew very low over my chimney tops and I could read every letter on the huge envelope. There appeared to be hundreds of lights and it was a sight we shall never forget as we saw it disappear over Chapel St. Leonards at the speed of an express train."

The eye-witness can be forgiven for perhaps over-estimating a little the speed of Hindenburg. Flying at a cruising speed of 75 mph, the airship was somewhat slower than, say, the Flying Scotsman, which had become the first train to reach 100 mph a couple of years before, but judging the speed of a flying object which another observer described as being *"larger than Ingoldmells village"* must have been difficult.

Chapel escaped German air raids during World War II, but did have a close encounter with one particular Heinkel Bomber in October 1940. The aircraft had been attempting to destroy the Rolls-Royce engine factory in Derby and had already dropped its payload (on Stanton Ironworks by mistake) when, following skirmishes with a Hurricane from 151 Squadron the badly damaged bomber glided to a halt on the beach at Chapel St. Leonards opposite the end of Trunch Lane. The five crew members were captured and the engines salvaged from the stricken craft. One of them is displayed in the Lincolnshire Aviation Museum at Tattershall.

The crew of a British Halifax bomber were not so fortunate a couple of years later. An engine fire caused irreversible damage to a wing leading to the plane crash landing near to Chapel. Four crew members died, and three others were badly injured. A memorial stone was laid in 2004. It can be seen off Langham Lane, near to Langham House Farm in Mumby village.

Allied or German planes flying overhead was a common sight in the years of the war. There was a single fatal attack in this part of Lincolnshire's coast. At Huttoft, three died, more were injured and buildings destroyed when a lone aircraft dropped four high explosive bombs in the afternoon of 10th January 1943. A plaque in Huttoft church commemorates the dead.

Should you wish to view some of the wartime defence systems used by the British Armed Forces, Chapel is a good place to visit. At Chapel Point, a large gun emplacement and viewing platform have been restored, with a helpful information board added, and several pillboxes can still be seen, including one between Chapel Point and Anderby Creek and another within the caravan park site at Anderby Creek.

In recent years, the village of Chapel St. Leonards has undergone something of a makeover. In 2008 a large, rather unusual bell tower was installed in the centre of the village green. It is most certainly a focal point, both visually and when it chimes on the hour, but opinions are divided – it is a bit too modern-looking for some. The green itself has been encircled with railings that complement similar along the nearby promenade. Solar lighting adds a subtle, and environment-conscious effect to the village after dark. If you want bouncy castles, amusement arcades, bingo and fast food, you'll find them all in Chapel, but you will also find leisurely nature walks and plenty of quiet corners – there really is something to suit all tastes, with the promise of more to come!

We mentioned Zeppelins just now. In the next chapter, we will take a much closer look.

Further Reading:

For more on the Lincolnshire Coastal Country Park visit:

http://www.lincstrust.org.uk/what-we-do/living-landscapes/coast-and-marshes

For up to date information about Chapel St. Leonards visit:

http://www.chapelstleonards.com/

M. Hill, The Casualties Were Small: Wartime Poetry and Diaries of a Lincolnshire Seaside Villager, Ambridge Books (2009)

P is for A Pair of Kings (one a chapel, the other a trawler)

We touched on the German use of Zeppelin airships briefly in the preceding chapter. Now we will return to this topic to examine a tragic event in Cleethorpes. News reports in World War I were at best sketchy, sometimes inaccurate and often heavily influenced by the War Ministry and its requirements to restrict coverage of events that might lead to a loss of morale. With this in mind, we will begin our story of events at the Kings Baptist Chapel with this report from the *Lincolnshire Echo* on Monday 3rd April 1916 under the headline "A WEEK-END OF UNUSUAL ACTIVITY":

"The total casualties reported as a result of the Zeppelin raids on the night of March 31 – April 1 now amount to killed 43, injured 66. Nearly 200 explosive and incendiary bombs were dropped. A Baptist chapel, three dwelling-houses, and two cottages were destroyed, and a Town Hall, four dwelling-houses, 35 cottages, and a tramcar shed were partially wrecked, but no military damage was caused."

Hold those last six words in your mind as you read on. The Baptist chapel was indeed Cleethorpes own Kings chapel. Built in 1910 between Alexandra Road and Oole Road (about 100 feet south of the present-day library and Tourist Information Centre) as a place of worship for the Baptist congregation formed in 1904, the chapel was being used as a temporary billet for the men of 'E' Company, part of the 3rd Battalion, Manchester Regiment. Although the 3rd Battalion had been mobilised and stationed in Cleethorpes since October 194, the men of 'E' company had only arrived in the town the day before the Zeppelin raid. The new arrivals were warned to expect air raid sirens at night, in fact, the alarm had been sounded for several days in succession, but without materialising into an attack. But on the night of 1st April at 1.30 am, a Zeppelin was sighted off the south-east coast and the alarm was rung once again. On this occasion, the Zeppelin commander, having been forced to abort his intended attack on London because of an issue with the airships engines, set his sights on Grimsby.

Having been spotted by searchlights and under anti-aircraft fire the commander chose to release all of his bombs early. A flare was the first seen to fall, landing near to the pier, closely followed by an enormous explosion as a bomb hit the chapel's slate roof and detonated. Much of the building was demolished at a stroke and many of the men inside died instantly. Men from "A" company, billeted in neighbouring shops received injuries from flying debris. Two more bombs struck. One hit a council office building and the other in residential Sea View Street, thankfully without further loss of life. Three men from "E" company had decided to stay up late and were playing cards in the cellar of the church. They came through the horror of the bombing physically almost unscathed.

As daylight emerged, the full horror of the raid dawned on survivors. In total, thirty-three men died and another 50 suffered injuries, many of them life-changing. Twenty-four of the men were buried in Cleethorpes Cemetery the following Tuesday with full military honours. A mourner described the scene:

"3 bands, 3 regiments … Chopin's Funeral March played most beautifully by 3rd Manchester's Band as we enter from three sides of square … What a scene! They faint one after another … poor souls, some husbands, some sons, and some brothers – one widow, married only six weeks … First military funeral I have attended – trust it will be the last"

(Reproduced from the website of Doctor Alan Dowling)

Four years later a large stone memorial was unveiled near to the grave site. It reads:

In Memoriam
N.C.O.'s & men 3rd Battalion The Manchester Regt
Who lost their lives whilst serving their country on April 1st 1916

Are you still holding on to those last six words from the newspaper article earlier? The youngest to die was just seventeen years old, another had only joined up earlier that week. Many others left widows and children in the midst of the most horrific war the world had known at the time. The Times newspaper even reported some elements of the attack but added that it occurred in *"a village of no military significance"*.

The Baptist congregation moved into premises on nearby Cambridge Street for the next six years until a temporary corrugated iron and wood building was erected on the site of the bombed church. In 1927, a new church was built, utilising some of the foundations of the devastated original structure. A modern hall was added more recently. On the wall is a simple green plaque (one of several that form a rather nice heritage trail around the town) embossed with the words "The original BAPTIST CHURCH was destroyed during a Zeppelin airship attack in 1916 when 311 members of the Manchester Regiment were killed on April 1st."

You may be wondering what became of the Zeppelin? With the propaganda machine in full flow the *Lincolnshire Echo* report from the 3rd April hinted strongly to its readers that a heroic chase had occurred and that a New Zealander, Lieutenant Brandon of the Royal Flying Corps had successfully bombed it and damaged it to such an extent that it had come down in the Thames estuary. The truth is somewhat different. Brandon did indeed engage with a Zeppelin, and may well have inflicted damage, but whether or not this was L22 cannot be stated with any degree of certainty. What is definite is that L22 continued to operate for another 12 months before being brought down over the Netherlands whilst engaged in a reconnaissance mission.

So, our first King was a chapel. The second is a trawler – the King Stephen. The skipper was a man named William Martin, and as you read on, you may be tempted to judge his actions. Of course, that is up to you, but all I will do is lay before you accounts and theories behind them and request that you try to understand this very difficult situation from all angles.

The King Stephen was a Grimsby fishing trawler of some 160+ tons unladen and Martin, at 44 years of age was an experienced fisherman and captain who spent much of his life working the North Sea and its dangerous waters. Martin had responded to distress signals before, so, during a fishing trip on the night of 1st February 1916, when flares were sighted Martin did not hesitate to steam towards them.

The sight that met Martin and his crew as the new day dawned was not what they were expecting. In the water was the wreck of an airship with 16 German crew members hanging on for their lives. This was in fact Zeppelin L19 under the command of Kapitänleutnant Odo Löwe. The airship had taken part in a massive raid on English towns and cities the previous night (31st January) – one of nine Zeppelins to bomb and kill 61 people, injuring more than 100 others in a few hours. L19 had bombed several sites in the Birmingham area, but like four of its sister ships, it was having reliability issues with its recently fitted Maybach engines. By the afternoon of 1st February Kapitänleutnant Löwe signalled that only one engine (out of four) was still operating and his radio was operating intermittently. At this time the airship was about 30 miles north of the Dutch coast.

L19 was a P-class Zeppelin, designed to carry a crew of 18 or 19, but it was not unusual during air raids when fully loaded with bombs to reduce crew size in order to save on weight. On this occasion Löwe was accompanied by 15 officers and men.

It should be mentioned that even up to this point in the story, accounts vary. In Admiral Reinhard Scheer's book *Germany's High Sea Fleet in the World War*, blame for the L19 coming down is attributed to foggy conditions leading to the airship flying over neutral Dutch territory and coming under fire. Reinhard described what happened next:

"Owing to the damage done, when it (L19) again came over the water it was unable to rise on account of a strong northerly wind and so was forced to come down at about 100 nautical miles from the English coast, in a line with Grimsby."

Whatever caused the airship to come down, down it was and William Martin faced an immediate and urgent dilemma. His trawler could carry sixteen more men, but these were military men, the enemy. And, they were carrying weapons. His crew of eight were fishermen, unarmed and unprepared for combat. Martin feared that if he rescued the airship's contingent, he could soon find his boat taken over and steaming for Germany. The skipper discussed his anxiety with mate George Denny who shared his concerns. William concluded that it would not be safe to bring the German men on board – a decision that would haunt him for the rest of his life.

Reinhard Scheer had become Commander of the High Seas Fleet the previous month. His response to William Martin was to call it a *"shameful* deed", in that he "*allowed the helpless crew to perish in the waves*". Martin later explained that he recorded the stricken airship's position so that he could send help should he come across any Royal Navy ships on his return journey. As things turned out, he reached his home port of Grimsby before he was able to report it.

In later interviews both Martin and Denny acknowledged the difficulty of leaving sixteen Germans to their fate – Denny recalled the cries of "*save us, save us*" from many of them, and being told by other crew members that shouts of "*may God punish England*" followed when the *King Stephen* turned away from the airship.

All sixteen of the L19's crew died in the water. A note written by Löwe and posted in a bottle was found by Swedish fishermen over 300 miles away later in the year. In it the airship's commander described the crews "*last hour*" as they floated "*on the top platform and backbone girder*" of the remains of their fallen Zeppelin. In early February water temperatures were likely to have been only a degree or two above freezing – hypothermia will develop in under an hour in such conditions, unconsciousness and death following on swiftly.

Since this chapter is titled "*A pair of Kings*" let us next consider the fate of the *King Stephen*. After returning to Grimsby it was commandeered by the Royal Navy and converted into a Q-ship. A tactic used by the navy was to conceal armaments in merchant ships in order to lure unsuspecting U-boats into attack. As many as 350 such Q-ships were used in the First World War in this way. Figures suggest that it was not a great success – some 14 U-boats were destroyed at a "cost" of over 60 Q-ships. Some have suggested that strategists effectively sacrificed Q-ships and their crews in order to divert U-boats from more militarily significant targets. This particular Q-ship engaged with a U-boat on 25 April 1916 and while chasing after it, the King Stephen ran straight into a German fleet returning from a bombardment of the East Coast. Torpedo boat G41, on its first operational engagement, made swift and effective use of one of its 500mm torpedoes, sinking the King Stephen in minutes.

Lieutenant Tom Phillips and his crew were captured and taken prisoner. When the German authorities released this ship was in fact the King Stephen, Phillips was charged with war crimes. It was some time before they realised the man they held was not, in fact, William Martin – it took a British newspaper photograph of the Grimsby man to identify him. The Lieutenant and his crew spent the remainder of the war as POW's in Germany.

William Martin was never the same man after the incident. Some described his actions as heroic, but in Germany, and in parts of Britain he was branded as a coward and murderer. Flight magazine described it as *"retribution"* for the *"Zeppelin pirates"* and gave all Germans *"a very stringent object lesson, of the estimate in which the word of the Germans is now held by civilised people"*. Newspapers around the world carried the story. The *Grey River Argus* in New Zealand said the *"Trawlers action"* was *"justified"* because of *"Hunnish Treachery"*. The *Western Times* might, at first glance appeared to be giving a balanced summary of opinion under the headline "TWO VIEWS". The paper acknowledged *"a storm of indignation"* in Germany but immediately countered what it called *"consummate effrontery"* describing the Germans as *"evil"* and *"not to be trusted"*. To be fair to all the press, the information they were working with was inaccurate. The Western Times, like other papers, believed at the time that when Martin and his crew had come across the L19 they were outnumbered by at least six to one, stating *"the officers and men of the Zeppelin numbered fifty at least. Over twenty were counted on the outside and others were heard knocking below"*. The real ratio of sixteen Germans to nine British only emerged several years later.

The Bishop of London, Arthur Winnington-Ingram, already an outspoken critic of the Germans, having called them *"baby killers"* the previous year, following the lethal shelling of the Yorkshire coast, urged the English people to *"stand by the skipper of the trawler"*. Putting responsibility firmly on the German nation, and in direct response to claims that Kapitänleutnant Löwe had given Martin assurances of a peaceful passage should Martin accept his crew on board, the Bishop added *"the chivalry of war had been killed by the Germans, and their word could not be trusted"*.

In March, the *Boston Guardian* passed on the news that Martin had *"received a cheque for £22 from admirers in South Africa, who approve his action in declining to rescue the distressed Germans"*.

None of this prevented Martin from receiving hate mail and death threats, from home and abroad. His Great-Grandson, Pat Thompson, interviewed in 2014 recalls being told stories of poisoned cigarettes and wine being delivered to the beleaguered skipper. William Martin was captain of a ship, his prime responsibility being the lives of his own crew and the care of his vessel – in that order. Thompson admitted that Martin's decision haunted him. He never went to sea again, drank heavily for a while and died from heart failure at the age of 45 the following year. In his obituary, the *Lincolnshire Echo* said that *"ever since the encounter he has been haunted by an obsession that German agents were attempting to take his life"*. His widow re-married later that year and his twenty-year-old son, a minesweeper, was bound over for six months after assaulting her. The court was told he *"smacked her face, kicked her, and dragged her into the street by her hair"*. The whole sorry business had taken its toll on more people than most realised.

There may have been another factor influencing Martin's decision-making. Allegations have surfaced that the King Stephen was fishing in a restricted zone. Admittance of such could have led to prosecution, even suspension of his licence and loss of his ship. Whether that is true or weighed on his conscience no human will ever know.

In a final twist, Mr Thompson acknowledged that his Great-Grandfather had almost certainly suffered with Post Traumatic Stress Disorder. He also said that he had recently visited the gravesite of Heinrich Specht, a crewmember of the crashed Zeppelin. Whilst there, speaking to the BBC, he said *"If I could make amends I would. All I can do is send my sincere apologies"*. However, shortly afterwards, in an interview with the *Yorkshire Post* newspaper he wrote *"I don't want great-grandad portrayed as a villain. Whatever he did, I'm sure he had his reasons. The trawlermen were unarmed. They were just working men"*.

So, if you were expecting *"a Pair of Kings"* to be a chapter about good fortune, you will have been very disappointed. Hopefully, the next one will make amends.

Further Reading:

Adm. R. Scheer, Germany's High Sea Fleet in the World War, Shilka (2013 paperback edition – also available online)

A. Dowling, Cleethorpes: The Creation of a Seaside Resort, Phillimore (2008)

Q is for "Quids in?" – the Quest to make money at the seaside

Walk down Mablethorpe High Street towards the sea and as you pass by the traffic lights and the indoor market on your left, you'd be forgiven for missing one of Lincolnshire's oldest and most interesting buildings. Simply called *"Bibby's Casino"* nowadays, this is the site of the once-famous *"Pie-in-Hand"*.

The building has a fascinating history. Opened in the second half of the nineteenth century, it took the name *Pie-in-Hand* when the owner, a man by the name of Duffin, purchased the figurehead from a stranded barge (the Renata – or Ronata). The story goes that Duffin negotiated a good price due to the figurehead having sustained some damage – something being held in one hand, most likely a bible had been broken off. Duffin nailed his purchase outside the restaurant with one significant addition. The figure now carried a pork pie instead of a bible. At the time, Duffin's establishment served a meal of pork pie with vegetables and a hot cup of tea for a shilling. It's hard to believe given modern-day regulations, but the Pie-in-Hand regularly catered for up to 200 diners at a time. On one occasion in 1897, a party of Diamond Jubilee revellers from Lincoln numbering over 400 took tea together!

It was a clever choice of name in a second way – Mablethorpe had a popular and successful hotel just alongside – the *"Book in Hand"*. The name is still in use as a public house, but much of the hotel building has been absorbed by the indoor market mentioned earlier. As for the Pie-in-Hand, this continued as café and boarding house until the middle of the 1920's when it undertook a transformation into a picture house, making the most of the boom in popularity of the cinema. Once again, to look at the building now, you'd struggle to envisage audiences of 300 or more enjoying a movie inside – the café was still boasting dining accommodation for up to 350 at this time. By the 1940's with towns awash with picture houses and the nation at war once again the *"Pie"* opted for a new filling and became a radio store and amusement centre.

In 1945, owner William Jackson placed this advertisement in the "For Sale" section of the *Lincolnshire Standard and Boston Guardian*:

"2 cinematograph machines, 16 mm,

complete with stand and arc lamps,

ex cinema, will make good toys, £15 each"

These *"good toys"* were the same type of projection systems that had led to several picture house fires over the previous decades! But what the advert reminds us is that many seaside traders will quickly adapt to changes in market conditions – selling up one business in order to invest in a new one. Jackson had been a wise investor, his picture house had drawn in thousands of paying visitors but the sign above the entrance **"admission free"** was the clever bit. Inside, over a period of years Jackson had built up a collection of slot machines placed strategically inside the foyer of his picture house. This *"penny arcade"* caught the attention of visitors to such an extent that the machines were earning more revenue than the movie trade.

But, what was the big attraction of these arcades which had begun springing up in the years immediately prior to the First World War? Basically, your *"penny"* bought you one of two things. Either a quick bit of entertainment on machines such as bagatelles, fortune-tellers, strength challenges and the like. Alternately, you could play slot machines in the hope of winning your money back and more besides.

Slot machines are always designed to win. That is not to say that individual players will never beat them, but a machine that loses money is faulty and will quickly be repaired or replaced. Depending on their location (regional laws vary) slot machines are programmed (yes, they are!) to pay out between 75% and 95% of all takings – and always have been. Put simply, if gamblers feed, say, £1000 into a slot machine over a period of time, the device will retain at least £50 and as much as £250. It is all very clever, really. Customers see machines regularly paying out and are lured into believing they can win. Those that do even make a point of telling everyone else how much they won. The losers (which is actually most people) just leave quietly, probably having had a good time, losing slowly and believing there will always be another, luckier day for them.

There is an old saying *"you pays your money and you takes your choice"*. This definitely applies to amusement arcades. I'm not trying to convince you one way or the other – the only food for thought I'll leave you with is that the UK National Lottery, by comparison pays back just 50% of takings to gamblers in its prize fund.

From the point of view of an independent trader, automated machines offered customers entertainment that could be paid for without the need for so many paid staff. Think about fairground stalls such as hook-a-duck, for example. Each stall required at least one paid hand – an amusement arcade generally needed a couple of staff supervising machines and someone else to work that all-important feature of every penny arcade – the change booth. Often with over 100 attractions to lure punters to part with their change, arcades like the Pie-in-Hand could rake money in without a massive wage bill.

Many of the earliest penny arcades were connected to the piers. Lincolnshire's two piers at Cleethorpes and Skegness were no exception. After all, the railway companies and other speculators needed to recoup their investments, but over time amusement arcades found homes close to the seafront in buildings often designed with different uses in mind. One example is the theatre. Concert halls were big business in Victorian times – Cleethorpes had two (one on the pier and the Alexandra), even though Grimsby, a mile or so up the road had a couple of its own. The Alexandra Theatre (on Alexandra Road, where else?) opened in 1896 and was immediately attracting large audiences. Business was so good that Dutch cellist Auguste Van Biene was persuaded to invest considerably at the turn of the century. Seating capacity was expanded and the theatre was renamed the Empire. Biene himself played his celebrated piece *The Broken Melody* on the opening night in June 1900. But, people *change* and *people* change. Over time, visitors sought different ways to entertain themselves at the seaside, and the seaside was attracting different kinds of people. By 1960, the Empire was forced to bing down the curtain for a final time.

What is it now? The building is fronted by large signs advertising *Fairworld Amusements* featuring indoor golf, lazer adventure and the prospect of £100+ jackpots. Being an indoor venue, open long hours, it attracts customers of all ages, whatever the weather. Perhaps this is why amusement arcades continue to fill up our seafronts. They are warm and dry, often play loud music and, as we have already seen, you don't have to pay a penny to step inside – most of them don't even have doors!

What has traditionally set seaside towns apart from inland towns and cities is the resilience and adaptability of its entrepreneurs. All this is beginning to change as the international fast food franchises muscle in amongst the family concerns that have often operated for generations. As we have seen, Cleethorpes Pier is currently being transformed into Britain's largest Fish and Chip restaurant. Only time will tell how this affects nearby local restaurants.

Some individuals have forged notable names for themselves with unusual forms of entertainment at the seaside. Take the case of Billy Daring, for example. Billy's act involved diving off Cleethorpes Pier into a metal tank of water. Not content with this as a spectacle, Billy set himself ablaze first. This particular stunt made it into the newspapers in July 1928 for all the wrong reasons:

> *"Billy Daring, who provides holidaymakers with a thrill by diving into a tank with his clothing ablaze, was badly burned when some of the petrol in which his clothes are soaked reached his skin."*

The *Hartlepool Northern Daily Mail* disclosed that matters got worse, as the unfortunate man struck his head on the tank, requiring medical attention for serious burns AND a nasty head injury. Billy was at least the third daredevil diver to perform stunts on the Lincolnshire coast. The first, and perhaps most famous was *"Professor"* Billy Thomason. *"Billy the Diver"* as he was known, performed at piers around the British Isles, but Skegness was his home. Billy used a 60-foot-high platform from which the one-legged diver would plunge into the sea in front of enormous crowds. The most dangerous of his dives involved being secured in a sack which was set alight before Billy leapt from his platform *"falling like a meteor"* into the sea. Thomason avoided bad accidents in his personal career, but did make it into the newspapers on a couple of occasions, for a different reason. In July 1911, Billy made several unsuccessful attempts to rescue a swimmer in distress. The man drowned in spite of Thomason diving several times off the Northern side of the pier. In September 1915 after

Billy had completed his show another gentleman persuaded officials to let him dive in as well. The man completed his dive but got into difficulties in the water. The *Skegness, Mablethorpe and Alford News* picks up the story:

"Billy ... dived into the water again and swam strongly to the swimmer, who, spent by his efforts to swim against the current, was well neigh exhausted. (He) was only just in time and had to support the visitor with one arm and keep himself going with the other arm and leg."

It took twenty minutes for a boat to reach the men and haul them both to safety.

Several of the daredevil divers that entertained by entering the sea in flames or on a bicycle were missing a limb, and often added the prefix *"Professor"* to their names. Billy Thomason's successor was no exception. Frank Gadsby was born in Nottinghamshire and lost his left leg above the knee at the age of four. By the time he was 12, Frank was such a strong swimmer that he had been invited to perform in front of King George V. In 1920, Frank took over from Thomason and began substituting *"Peggy"* in place of his forename. A new feature of Peggy's act involved diving into a blazing water tank 5 metres across, filled with only 5 feet of water – we have seen already, the dangers of such a dive. Over time, the act expanded to include Franks two sons, Leslie and Kenneth and became known as the *"Aqua Trio"*. Leslie lost a hand in an accident with an exploding flare whilst performing on the west coast in 1931, and narrowly avoided death when blown off course during a dive at Glasgow's Empire Exhibition of 1938. Gadsby missed his intended target – a metal water tank and fell heavily from 20-feet to the ground. Amazingly, he was declared fit to resume diving later the same day. Leslie was still taking his diving show around the country well into his forties. Peggy died in 1958 at the age of 79, at his home in Nottinghamshire.

Were these daredevil performers quids-in from their crowd-pulling stunts. All I know is that the Gadsby family did not make enough money from it to give up running a scrap-metal business in Skegness at the same time.

Earning a living at the seaside is, and always has been, hard work. Whether it involves providing accommodation for holidaymakers, feeding them, or keeping them entertained, as the saying goes "there's no gain without pain". We have just touched on a few examples here to illustrate the point. Thousands of people make their living from the fact that even greater numbers enjoy visiting the Lincolnshire coast year in year out. Now we will look back in time at some visitors that came and went, but left their mark.

Further Reading:

V. Mitchell, Branch Lines to Skegness & Mablethorpe, Middleton Press (2016)

M. Fey, Slot Machines: A Pictorial History, Liberty Belle (1994)

R is for Reports of Romans

As we saw earlier in our look at Gibraltar Point, Wainfleet has a long history. Once a busy coastal sea port, archaeological evidence has been used to suggest that this was in fact a Roman settlement known by the Latin name of *Vainona*.

William Stukeley was born in Holbeach in 1687, the son of a lawyer. He had a successful early career practicing medicine in Boston before becoming a priest at Stamford. By this time, Stukeley was already a Fellow of the Royal Society and a member of the Society of Antiquaries, an organisation under Royal Charter since 1751 to foster *"the encouragement, advancement and furtherance of the study and knowledge of the antiquities and history of this and other countries"*.

A contemporary, and good friend, of Isaac Newton, Stukeley was one of the earliest to record the famous account of the *"falling apple"*. He also worked with Edmund Halley, the renowned astronomer and was one of the first to describe how the earth *"wobbles"* slightly around its polar axis. One of William's principal archaeological interests was in the Roman influence on Britain, and particularly his home county of Lincolnshire.

What can be said with some certainty is that Stukeley studied the area around Wainfleet intently in the early 1720's. His findings were published within the first volume of his *"account of the antiquities, and remarkable curiosities in nature or art, observed in travels through Great Britain"*. In this, he became the first to equate the Roman town of Vainona with Wainfleet. He wrote *"for I am certain it (Wainfleet) is the Vainona mentioned by the famous author of Ravenna who has happily preserved so many of our British cities"*. The *Ravenna* referred to by Stukeley was a compendium of place names assembled by an unknown cleric in the Italian city of the same name in the eighth century. Here is where the first area of doubt creeps in. The Ravenna Cosmography as it is commonly known, is notoriously difficult to interpret. The source text contained many notable errors and series of mistranslations led to further rogues creeping in. However, when William Stukeley visited Wainfleet he met people who *"say there is a road across the East Fen, called Salter's Road* which probably was the Roman road; and there are people now alive who knew such as had remembered it." Stukeley concluded that "this was the place where the Romans made their salt of the sea water, to supply all this province; and it is not improbable that this road led to Banovallum (Horncastle), Lindum (Lincoln) &c.". In support of his judgement, William noted that "many salt hills are visible from Wainfleet to Friskney". William Stukeley was a studious man, well-read and much-travelled, he was convinced that Wainfleet was once a Roman settlement, but do his claims stand up to closer scrutiny?

 Edmund Oldfield published a *detailed topographical and historical account of Wainfleet and the Wapentake of Candleshoe, in the County of Lincoln* in 1829. From the outset, Oldfield attributed much of Wainfleet's topography to Roman intervention. For example, he described a bank "upon a ridge of high land, which enters the wapentake at Friskney, and runs nearly in a straight line ... to the present haven, about a quarter of a mile below the town of Wainfleet All Saints" which he credited to "enterprising Romans ... impelled, no less by their love of agriculture, than by their desire to deprive the Britons, of these secure, and to the Roman legions, almost inaccessible places of retreat". This raised line can still be seen, and, in fact, to the north at Ingoldmells it retains the name "Roman Bank". More recent archaeological surveys including one conducted by Network Archaeology in 2004 have concluded the embankment to be much more recent, most probably from the Saxon period of the fifth century onwards. Other finds, such as human bones, in the vicinity of Wainfleet point to the area being worked for its salt as much as 1,500 years before the Roman occupation of Britain. The process of harvesting salt by evaporating sea water was used by the Romans at various sites along the East coast including several in nearby Norfolk, but the practice was dying out by the third century.

Several hauls of roman coins and pottery fragments have been unearthed over the years, pointing at some form of sustained Roman presence in the area. The Romans had significant settlements in Horncastle, Ulceby and Caistor, where they exploited the fertile agricultural lands of the Lincolnshire Wolds. It is possible that Wainfleet was Vainona as Stukeley suggested, but for me, two factors make this unlikely. Firstly, Wainfleet was on the coast at the time and, if used as a port by the Romans, surely this would be documented somewhere. Secondly, and perhaps, more importantly, the Romans were prolific road builders. If Wainfleet was an active port and source of salt for the Romans in Britain, then some evidence of a road connecting the town with Horncastle or Boston would be evident and it is not (yet!).

So, we simply do not know for sure if Wainfleet is really a Roman town, but don't let that put you off spending a little time there. It has much to offer as we shall see as we take a short tour around this remarkable little town.

Sir Edward Barkham, a sixteenth century London leather dealer, made so much money in City dealings that he bought large areas of land in Norfolk and South Lincolnshire – including Wainfleet. The manor stayed in the Barkham family (also heavily involved with the East India Company) until the second half of the eighteenth century, at which point the Wainfleet area was gifted to "the incurables of Bethlem Hospital". The psychiatric hospital in London was quick to realise the economic potential of the area and set about improving the salt marsh embankments and developing residential areas in the town with a view to raising a regular income through a lettings scheme.

With several properties falling into disrepair, funds were set aside for new buildings and in 1847, under the wings of prominent London architect Sydney Smirke RA, Barkham Street was born. Walk down this grand, wide avenue of 19 tall houses and you'd be forgiven for thinking you were in Southwark – since the same architect built several blocks of houses to the same specification there too. To think, in 1850 you could have rented one of these four bedroomed houses for the princely sum of £12 per annum. Perhaps even harder to believe as you stroll down this beautiful row, is that the whole lot cost just £7,500 to build – the entire street is now Grade II Listed.

Two more listed buildings are to be found in the market square, just a short walk to the south of Barkham Street. You cannot fail to spot the grand clock tower. It has kept time in the town since May 1899. Most local people refer to it as the clock or the tower, but its full title is the Walter Martin Memorial Clock Tower. The unfortunate Mr Martin, was a well-known farmer, estate agent, land valuer and local councillor. He was also one of the trustees of the aforementioned Bethlem hospital. He died in Skegness in 1896 at just 38 years of age following complications after a tooth extraction. He left a widow and three children. Plaques on three sides identify the clock tower with various members of the Martin family. The second listed structure in the market square is the fifteenth century limestone butter cross. The iron work at the top and weather vane are much more recent, with the stone obelisk standing on three steps and being a distinctive octagonal pillar. Many English market towns have their own butter crosses, the name supposedly originating from the fact that they denoted a market where basic commodities such as butter would be for sale. Wainfleet's is also associated with John Wesley, a Lincolnshire man himself, who is said to have preached what was to become Methodism here during the eighteenth century. When you look at the butter cross and clock tower standing almost side by side in what is now a public car park for much of the week, it is hard to imagine that a market has operated here since Henry de Lacy, the third Earl of Lincoln was granted a charter for such a purpose in 1282 by his close friend Edward Longshanks.

Remaining in the Market Square, three inns are worth mentioning. The one in the square itself, the Woolpack is nowadays a focal point for Bateman's brewery – of which more shortly, but in the seventeenth century it was the home of the prominent mercer, John Shaw. A mercer being a merchant in fabrics including wools, you can see where the name came from. In fact, the inn was almost certainly called the Mercer's Arms prior to taking on its present name. Just along the road from the Woolpack are the Red Lion and the Angel, the latter once being the residence of the Barkham family. The Red Lion is at least 220 years old, and may well be considerably older. What stood before these inns is not clear, but in 1829, whilst digging in the cellar of the Angel Inn, Roman earthenware was uncovered.

Wainfleet apparently gets its name from two words wegn and fleot. The latter is found in old English and Norse and has been used to mean "float", or an inlet of water or "creek". The former is less common but is generally taken to mean a wagon. So wegnfleot was a place where a carriage could cross or ford a stream. The Steeping River does in fact pass through Wainfleet, but a thousand years ago, it also met the sea here.

Although mention of it is found in the Domesday book, William Patten is credited by most as being the man who put Wainfleet on the map, so to speak. William was born in the town at the very end of the fourteenth century and, as William Waynflete, he had a long and varied career. By the age of 30, he was headmaster of Winchester College. In his eleventh year at Winchester, William was introduced to King Henry VI who was so taken up with the man that he appointed him to the most senior administrative position of Provost at his newly founded college in Oxfordshire – Eton. Waynfletes' stock with the King was so strong that in 1447 when the Bishop of Winchester died, his nephew Henry immediately replaced him with William. From his position as Bishop, Waynflete established a new college at Oxford, which he named St. Mary Magdalene after a hospital of the same name in Winchester which he had overseen in his earlier career. Subsequently he became Lord Chancellor, principal adviser to the King himself.

William's legacy in his birth town was Magdalene College, which he founded as a kind of feeder school to his Oxford University College. The magnificent building functioned as a school until the 1930's and is until recently was home to Wainfleet's own library and museum. The future of these facilities is in serious doubt due to financial cutbacks, however, as a Grade I listed building the twin-towered red brick structure has a more certain destiny.

In September 1867, the following auction notice appeared in the *Stamford Mercury*:

"Lot 3 A close of rich Arable Land containing 4A 0R 4P (more or less), bounded by lands of Sir Atwell King Lake, Bart, north-east, and lands of Mr John Pinder west. In the occupation of Mr. George Bateman".

The tenancy was being sold by Bateman to raise revenue for a project that had been taking shape in his mind for some time – Bateman had farmed sheep on his land at Friskney for some time, but wanted to turn his dream of being a brewer into a reality. Eight years later having agreed a deal with Edwin Crowe to buy out the lease of his Wainfleet brewery, Bateman took the plunge and relinquished the remaining 90% of his farm holdings. Crowe had been brewing in Wainfleet for many years and knew his craft well, as did his chief brewer, a man who was rapidly losing his sight.

Fortunately for Bateman and his wife, the pair were happy to pass on their brewing knowledge and wisdom to the enthusiastic couple. The "South End" brewery was close to the new railway line but by 1880 the business was going so well that Bateman was able to purchase "Salem House" a couple of hundred yards away. The large Georgian property included coaching houses which George converted into a new brewery.

The Bateman family moved into brewing in a most challenging period for the industry. A rapidly emerging trend was for larger specialist breweries serving wider areas than the smaller independent brewers. Between 1870 and the onset of the first world war, two thirds of the smaller breweries had disappeared, replaced by industrial giants producing half a million barrels or more every year. In a little over ten years towards the end of the nineteenth century Lincolnshire alone lost nearly half of its breweries.

Bateman's has endured through two world wars and prolonged periods of economic depression. In the 1930's Lincolnshire was home to sixteen independent breweries, by the 1980's just a handful remained. The situation is improving as the modern trend for micro-breweries continues and the number has risen to the levels of eighty years ago. In Wainfleet, Bateman's brewery operates from Salem Mill and a new building "the theatre of beers", opened in 2002. Tours of the brewery are popular attracting visitors from all over the world.

To conclude our tour of this remarkable little town, let's return to the corner of High Street and Barkham Street and a building that might normally escape the attention of passer's-by, the *Coronation Hall*. Plans for a hall to honour the coronation of King George V in June 1911 were finalised the following year and the building was completed in just twelve months. Princess Marie Louise of Schleswig-Holstein, grand-daughter of Queen Victoria accepted an invitation to open the new hall. The *Lincolnshire Echo* gave considerable coverage to the occasion on Saturday 27th September 1913 – and provided a little local history lesson to boot:

GREAT DAY AT WAINFLEET

CORONATION HALL OPENED

BY PRINCESS MARIE LOUISE

"Wainfleet, an old world town of East Lincolnshire ... is nothing if not patriotic ... When England's right on the high seas was threatened by the dreaded Spanish Armada, Wainfleet was not behindhand. The sturdy yeomen of the town and district made themselves responsible for two ships and six hundred men – a very considerable and useful offer in those troublous times."

The newspaper informed readers that the £600 cost of the new hall had been found by a combination of generous public and private subscription. Throughout the previous year, a succession of flower shows, garden fetes, decorated vehicle parades and the like had all helped swell funds. In addition, the governors of Bethlem Hospital (who, remember, owned the properties on neighbouring Barkham Street, offered the site for free with just a nominal annual rent for a period of 99 years. As you pass by the building the newspapers description of it may be helpful:

"The building is of attractive appearance, being eighty feet long and twenty-seven feet wide ... The front is on the old style, being pebble-dashed and possessing parapet walls. It is handsomely fitted up inside, and has a stage of some magnitude with a fine proscenium. There are closing shutters, so that it can be converted into a room if required, while the ante-rooms are also nicely furnished."

Giving her public address from the platform inside the hall, the Princess disclosed a feeling that Wainfleet had "a claim" on her. She explained with the following reasons:

"on account of its historical interest, and on account of the fact that William of Waynflete founded Magdalen College (where) my eldest brother was a student."

Marie Louise was referring to Edward Albert, the Prince of Wales – generally known by the name of David.

The Coronation Hall is still in full-time use as a public venue. It has been home for various productions of the Wainfleet Drama Society, countless fayre's, dances and bazaars as well as wedding receptions and the like. As a venue, capable of holding up to 200 guests, Wainfleet with its population of under 2,000 is very well served.

Wainfleet may or may not have some Roman heritage, but it is very much a town worthy of a much closer look. Something of a secret gem some might say, as are our next ports of call.

Further Reading:

W. Stukeley, An account of the antiquities, and remarkable curiosities in nature or art, observed in travels through Great Britain, London (1776), Available to read freely online at:

https://archive.org/details/bub_gb_HphaAAAAYAAJ

E. Oldfield, A *detailed topographical and historical account of Wainfleet and the Wapentake of Candleshoe, in the County of Lincoln*, London (1826), Available to read freely online at:

https://archive.org/details/atopographicala00oldfgoog

S is for the Saltfleetby – Theddlethorpe Dunes, Sutton-on-Sea and other Secret Gems

A little way south of Mablethorpe you will find Sutton-on-Sea, a lovely seaside village with a population similar to that of Wainfleet. Somewhat confusingly, the village has gone by the names of Sutton-le-Marsh or Sutton-in-the-Marsh, sometimes simultaneously.

For example, in 1882, the *Boston Guardian* printed a list of visitors to the Bacchus Hotel, Sutton-le-Marsh, in 1888, the *Stamford Mercury* advertised an auction taking place beside the same hotel at Sutton-on-Sea, and the same newspaper listed details of an auction at Sutton-in-the Marsh just a few years earlier. It gets more complicated. In some circles the village went by the name of Sutton West Alford for a while.

Some might describe Sutton as the village that once was, while others might call it the dock that never was. Let me explain. Parts of the Lincolnshire coastline have suffered terribly from the effects of erosion over the centuries. Sutton a thousand years ago, was a small village roughly a mile to the east of where it is now – almost entirely now under water. Locals occasionally say that on very low tides, evidence of the drowned village can still be seen. As for Sutton docks? Towards the end of the nineteenth century proposals were made to establish a large dock site at Sutton-on-Sea, connected to the rest of the country by extending the existing rail network. In the short term, a steam tram line was established connecting the village with Alford, but the rail and docks proposals never made it through parliament and the tram line closed down after just a handful of years, initially announcing a temporary closure for the winter months in 1889, but never actually reopening. As for the railways, Sutton did get a branch line and railway station connecting passengers with nearby Willoughby and Mablethorpe. This remained in use until 1970. The railway line was torn up the following year. The only evidence that a station ever existed in Sutton is the name of *"The Sidings"* given to a residential road built over the remains of the old line. If you look at an aerial photograph, you can just make out the path of the line running NNW from Sutton-on-Sea towards Mablethorpe. I doubt that modern residents and business folk who make their living from tourism regret the decision not to build docks at their seaside village.

Sutton-on-Sea is in fact a very popular retirement destination. So much so that over 60% of the population are either pensioners or within 10 years of pensionable age. Even the village's own website calls it *"the resort for quiet holidays"*, going on to recommend it for *"a relaxing holiday"* or *"a place to settle down after a busy life"*. Property, therefore commands premium prices. Even the beach huts are expensive. A brick built hut on Bohemia Promenade will set you back at least £17,000, but you will get free car parking all year round and free use of the public toilets 50 yards away!

One thing to keep your eye open for in the event of very low tides (but be careful walking on the beach – the tide can come back in very quickly) is what people call the *"buried forest"*. As we have mentioned the coastline has changed dramatically over time. In fact, some 7,000 years ago, dry land and forest stretched out over what is now the North Sea for several miles. Gradually as the sea encroached and swallowed up the forest all evidence of it disappeared beneath layers of peat and other sediments below the water. But, times change, and the erosive power of the waves in the last century or so, have been wearing these sediments away so that from time to time a bizarre array of semi-fossilised (or perhaps petrified is more appropriate) tree trunks and stumps become exposed again – it really is a strange and fascinating sight.

Sutton-on-Sea has at times become Sutton-beneath-the-Sea. The two most noteworthy occasions being in 1571 when storm force winds whipped up an already exceptionally high tide and much of the village and its church was washed away. More recently, in January 1953, another storm forced the sea to rise over ten feet higher than normal. The consequences for Sutton were devastating. Sea defences at a place later named Acre Gap were completely destroyed and a cocktail of saltwater, mud and sand rushed into the village, flooding streets and properties. Many people were forced to evacuate their homes, for some it was several months before they could return. The row of seafront beach huts was badly damaged and the whole of the bowling green and lily pond behind was completely flooded.

One of the consequences of upgrading sea defences in the wake of the 1953 flood is that the entire coastline between Sutton and Mablethorpe is now protected by a sea wall topped with a promenade offering a lovely walk or cycle ride. In fact, in the opposite direction, most of the coastline to Skegness is also protected by a concrete wall in similar fashion so that more than three quarters of the fifteen-mile stretch between Mablethorpe and Skegness can be walked without the risk of getting your feet wet!

The same cannot be said if you visit the Saltfleetby-Theddlethorpe Dunes. This National Nature Reserve encompasses four square miles of dunes, wetlands, marshes and seashore stretching from the northern end of Mablethorpe to Saltfleet almost five miles away. A public footpath running parallel to the coastline follows the western perimeter of the reserve.

This is a fascinating place to study wildlife as dunes, saltmarshes and freshwater marshes all attract different species, yet can all be found within a few paces of one another. This is a dynamic landscape in that it is constantly changing. Studies are showing that dunes along the southern end of the reserve are forming and growing allowing scientists to study the development of these fascinating coastal features in real-time. At the northern end, the dunes are much older. The seaward dunes are relatively new, having formed during the eighteenth century following a scheme to divert the path of the *Great Eau*. This chalk-stream river does not take its name from the French word for water as you might expect, but from the short old English word *Ea* meaning *"river"*. On the landward side, the second row of dunes are much older, probably forming after storm surges in the thirteenth century. Between the two sets of dunes sits a considerable freshwater marsh, sheltered from both the prevailing south-westerly wind and the volatile east wind that sometimes brings storms and floods to the area.

An abundance of wildlife attracts people from all over the world – some of them venturing out after dark in search of the nocturnal natterjack toad, considered to be very rare in these parts. This is also a home or stopping-off point for many different groups of migrant birds. As a result, especially in the winter months many different birds of prey can be seen here picking off wading birds as they feed on the exposed shore.

The reserve is well sign-posted and has several places where car parking is available, but is also easily accessed on foot from nearby Mablethorpe. Please pay attention to the public notices as some areas are designated as sanctuary sites and are therefore off-limits. A further section is restricted as this is owned by the Ministry of Defence and was formerly used as a bombing range. Management of the reserve is in the hands of Natural England as well as the Lincolnshire Wildlife Trust. Both organisations provide free literature and run free events throughout the year. A feature of the site is the *Rimac Trail*. This is a very slightly sloping but fully accessible trail in a figure-of-eight loop of about 900 yards in total length. The trail takes in two viewing platforms, one with panoramic views of the saltmarsh and a second overlooking a large pond, teeming with wildlife. Three more trails, the coastguard trail, the Seaview trail and the Churchill Lane trail are all waymarked and allow visitors to take in every aspect of this fascinating reserve.

The area has attracted nature lovers for well over a century. As long ago as 1893 in an article compiled by members of the Lincolnshire Naturalists Union for the *Lincolnshire Chronicle* newspaper it was described as an area *"full of interest, no less to the botanist than the zoologist"*. Visitors were informed that *"the dunes are thickly sprinkled with thickets of the sea buckthorn, dewberry, sloe and binding grass and sedge"*. Nearby the authors observed wild garlic as well as *"wild celery, the great water parsnip, the early marsh orchids"* and, *"on the salt marsh, near Saltfleet, the rare Scirpus"*. Records dating back to 1895 show that efforts were being made by the local authorities to protect the birds in this region from hunters.

If seclusion is your preference, but you also want a lovely sandy beach then a trip a couple of miles south of Sutton-on-Sea is to be recommended. If you thought Sutton was peaceful, wait until you find Mogg's Eye. You can park a car beside a wide sandy beach and, at many times of the year, have it all to yourselves. Don't expect much in the way of facilities, and, if you intend swimming, be aware that there are no lifeguard patrols here, but if you are looking for somewhere off the beaten track with beautiful views, particularly as the Sun comes up over the sea first thing in the morning, then this is a place that you'll find hard to beat.

Just a half-mile to the south of Mogg's Eye is the hamlet of Anderby Creek. This has a unique feature – a cloud bar. No, it doesn't serve drinks. Rather, it is a focal point for observing, identifying and following cloud formations. Designed by Michael Trainor, a member of the Cloud Appreciation Society (Yes, there really is one!) the facility is built on the site of a run-down beach shelter. The clever thing is that by using movable mirrors, you can track your favourite clouds across the sky, without having to stand up or to crane your neck. Be prepared to spend more time there than you might have expected, and plan your visit to coincide with a day where the sky is a mixture of sunshine and clouds – when the centre opened in 2009, the sky was a beautiful, uninterrupted blue almost all day! Make sure to read the very helpful information boards – these will help you to identify the ten most common cloud types and to understand basic principles of cloud formation.

It might surprise you to find that Anderby Creek, home to 5 caravan sites and a chalet park, markets itself as *"unspoilt"*, but it is a fair description for two reasons. Firstly, the area is covered by a protection order prohibiting the installation of amusement arcades and the like, and secondly, its wide expanse of sandy beach and grassy dunes provides plenty of room for holidaymakers to find their own pitch on the sands. In 2014, the BBC's Good Beach Guide gave Anderby Creek the accolade *"the perfect place to get away from the crowds"*.

The tiny village of Anderby is just half a mile inland from the Creek, connected via the appropriately named *"Sea Road"*. It's most infamous resident was a man by the name of Thomas Hewson, who became well known in these parts, particularly around Skegness, as a prolific smuggler. Hewson, a tailor by his official trade, was also suspected, but never convicted, of being a murderer. A young man from Sloothby disappeared, and his body was never recovered. The spotlight fell on Hewson when he was apprehended carrying the young lad's watch. Hewson was convicted for smuggling on several occasions, even having three boats seized and cut in half, but nothing seemed to deter him from what was then a lucrative, if illegal, trade.

Our final stopover in this tour of secret gems is a place that only exists because of the 1953 flood. With an urgent need to repair and renew sea defences, clay was extracted from several coastal sites including one at Wolla Bank, a mile to the south of Anderby Creek. This area is now a beautiful reedbed and pit, in the care of Lincolnshire Wildlife Trust. Access to the reedbed itself is restricted, as much for public safety reasons as for conservation needs – some of the pools are quite deep and obscured by reeds. Visitors can get a very good view, however, from the public car park and from a dedicated bird hide situated among the dunes at the northern end of the site. Two varieties of warbler nest here, as do reed bunting and whitethroats. Short-eared owls are often spotted in the winter months and marsh harriers can usually be seen in springtime.

These places of peace and tranquillity are much sought-after by folk living in Lincolnshire's large urban settlements. Let us turn our attention now to some of the industry in one of them.

Further Reading:

A free guide to the National Nature Reserve can be downloaded from *Natural England* at:

http://publications.naturalengland.org.uk/publication/38015

G. Dow, The Alford & Sutton Tramway, Oakwood Press (1947)

T is for Trades, some Traditional, others Temporary

The world of commerce changes increasingly rapidly. Just take a look through the annual list of Lincolnshire's top 100 businesses and you'll find several that didn't even exist twenty years ago. With that in mind, let's take just one coastal town – Boston – and have a look at some of its most successful, and strange, business operations of the last two hundred years.

Walk down Wormgate in Boston and you'd be forgiven for missing the original site of Jakeman's confectioners. Now one of Britain's leading producers of menthol based "soothing" boiled sweets, production has continued unceasingly in the Lincolnshire town since 1907. The factory is now located in a nearby industrial park – the business forced into an expanded premises as production swelled from 16 tonnes every week to over 17 tonnes every day – that's well over a million bags of menthol sweets every single week. The business was started as a family concern by Henry Jesse Jakeman, employing just a handful of people – now the workforce is over 50 people (and rising at a time when most businesses are actually contracting) and sales abroad, including lucrative markets in the United States, Germany, Ireland and the Middle East, look set to overtake home sales for the first time.

It is the menthol sweets that Jakeman's is famous for, but the company has sold other types of confectionery in the past. An advertisement in the Lincolnshire Standard and Boston Guardian in 1955 promoted Chocolate Eclairs, Blackcurrant & Raspberry Drops and Extra Strong Mints – all at 9d a quarter (4p in "new" money). In 1933, *old fashioned barley sugar, golden butter mints and clear ice mints* were *on sale everywhere* at 4d (1.5p) per quarter pound. For a while the business was even selling what it called "Boston Rock and Skittle Rock", proudly boasting to be "the only local makers". By the way, the company was still using the apostrophe in those days, and being a bit of a traditionalist myself, I can't get out of the habit, so it will remain as Jakeman's in this book at least.

The same newspaper carried an advert in 1917 showing that the "confectionery works" was, at that time, also selling raw materials direct to the public:

"JAM MAKING: If you require Good Keeping Jams, use only LIQUID AMERICAN GLUCOSE, as used by all leading Preserve Manufacturers. It will repay you. Half Sugar and Half Liquid Glucose, and good results. The right Glucose can be obtained at Jakeman's Confectionery Works, Boston".

Jakeman was a canny businessman, selling on everything that arrived in his factory, from glucose jars to sugar packets. As soon as something became surplus to requirements he put it up for sale in the local newspaper, from bicycles to freezers. By the time of his death in a London nursing home in February 1937 the little family business had made him financially comfortable enough to own a five-bedroomed house in Woodhall Spa and to have made multiple business trips across the Atlantic – he left over £19,000 in his will – a considerable amount in those days.

After Henry's death, the business passed into the hands of the White family. Under the stewardship of Wilfred and later his son, Herbert White, the company endured the difficulties of the Second World War and the post-war rationing period – sugar, for example, was not derationed until 1953. In 2007, Jakeman's became part of the "Lanes Health" family and is now worth more than £5 million (2015 accounts). A far cry from the days of 1938 when the business became a private company issuing a grand total of 2,500 £1 shares.

The Jakeman's story has a spicy twist to it. The proprietor of the business was actually a man by the name of Archibald Murray according to a 1921 account in the *Boston Guardian*. In a detailed description of a lengthy court case heard at the Boston Borough Police Court, the relationship between the two men was reported *"Archibald Murray, Proprietor of a business in Wormgate, Boston, maker of sweets, and Henry Jakeman, who was associated with him in the business"*.

For completeness sake, I should also point out that the site of Jakeman's factory is often recorded as Red Lion Street rather than Wormgate – simply due to the building being on the junction of the two roads in what is the oldest part of Boston. The Wormgate site undergoing several extensions and alterations over the years as business grew.

The White family also had a finger in another Boston pie – label printing. Wilfred's oldest son, Francis, being director in a label printing company (Suttertons) for a while. However, modern-day computer-printed labels are a very distant cousin to the kind invented by John Fisher, a tailor by trade. Fisher's timing was impeccable. The 1850's were a time of rapid expansion in the railways, with an ever-increasing amount of people and goods being transported. The East Lincolnshire Railway had recently opened a line connecting Boston with Louth and Grimsby. Spotting that paper luggage labels were fragile, easily torn or displaced from the items they were meant to identify, John came up with a fabric label with two distinctive features. Firstly, a metal eyelet through which string could be passed overcame the problem of labels becoming separated, and secondly, Fishers labels were folded over at two corners – a shape, now instantly recognizable, but which was unique to his business at the time.

John quickly realised that he could not cope with demand and took on a partner, George Clark, the son of a bookbinder, and originally a Londoner. Clark was young and energetic and quickly built up a very successful business, buying the label's inventor out of the company in 1876 shortly before his 39th birthday. George himself died a couple of years later at the age of 41, leaving a wife and eight children. The eldest, another George, just seventeen, took on what was by now called Fisher Clark supported by two of his brothers, Charles and Ernest. The business boomed, even Queen Victoria was a customer. By the 1880's Fisher Clark was selling pre-printed paper bags and cloth flour bags all over the country, as well as the ever-popular luggage tags. Charles passed away in 1898, at just 36 years old at a time when the business had outgrown its premises on Grove Street and was preparing to take on a new factory in nearby Norfolk Street.

By the 1930's, and several expansions of the factory later, Fisher Clark was employing 350 staff – one of Boston's largest firms, and sold a range of cloth and paper labels, tags and tickets, included gummed labels – the forerunner to self-adhesive labels. In 1960, Fisher Clark joined the Norcros Group and subsequently became part of Norprint International, a global operation with an annual turnover in excess of £50 million. In turn, the business was absorbed by Magnadata – built on the supply of magnetic tickets for public transport services including British Rail.

All good things come to an end, they say. In 2015, after more than 160 years operating in Boston, the business was forced to close its doors for good after Magnadata brought in the administrators. In the first half of its lifetime, Fisher Clark had employed a predominately female staff. Another business that did the same was the Boston Steam Laundry.

In the nineteenth century, many women earned a living working from home taking in washing for private clients. Women built up trade by developing a strong reputation with clients and allowing word of mouth and personal recommendation to develop new business. But this all changed in 1884 when the women of Boston suddenly found they had a commercial competitor. With an initial investment of £2000, a former cigar factory in Bond Street became the new home for a laundry business on an industrial scale. Rather than relying on word-of-mouth to attract trade, the new business paid for newspaper advertisements such as this one from the *Boston Guardian* of April 1887:

"ORDINARY WASHING and all kinds of LAUNDRY WORK (including CURTAINS) executed in FIRST CLASS STYLE at the same prices as those NOW CHARGED for Laundry work in Boston.

Arrangements can be made with families, Hotels, Schools or other large establishments at per dozen or per 100 articles, or per week, as may be agreeable to customers."

Intending customers were assured that a personal visit would be made by the forewoman to make arrangements and that *"goods are carefully packed in covered baskets and are fetched and delivered by the company's van"*. By 1897, the business was reporting annual profits in excess of £400 – a tidy sum. But it had not been easy. Just two years after establishing its premises on Bond Street, during the night of 9th September 1886, fire tore through the factory, and although the steam engine room was saved, around £300 worth of laundry was lost. Undeterred, the building was rebuilt, customers compensated and work resumed just three months later – in fact within two more years the business had expanded to take in nearby Skegness as well.

The Boston Steam Laundry certainly had an impact on the ability of many women to earn a living from home, but it also provided employment for several. As recently as 1954, the business was recruiting *"young women for laundry work"* by placing ads in the *Lincolnshire Standard and Boston Guardian*.

Modernisation was a cornerstone of the business – even in it's infancy, proudly boasting that the fire of 1886 had given it the opportunity to upgrade to better machinery. In 1928 the Laundry announced *"a new venture"*, the installation of a *"new water-softening apparatus"*, anticipating that the *"softer water will tend to prolong the existence of the linen and other materials"*.

Perhaps their best advertisement came in October 1938, and coincided with the first screening of Walt Disney's *Snow White and the Seven Dwarfs* at the Odeon Cinema in the town. To be fair, several other businesses had similar campaigns. The Steam Laundry ad read *"Why be GRUMPY? When the Boston Steam Laundry can make you HAPPY by doing your laundry quickly, efficiently and at reasonable prices. To do it yourself, it makes you SNEEZY, SLEEPY and DOPEY and leads to bringing in the DOC … Even if you're so BASHFUL our laundry service will be of great help to you by returning your sheets and linens SNOW WHITE"*.

Business continued, enduring the war years and the post-war period of economic austerity, but increasing competition during the 1960's led to trade with the Boston Steam Laundry drying up completely and the company was wound up in 1971. Not a trace of the original factory remains.

Just around the corner from Bond Street is Pipe Office Lane – just about the only surviving evidence of a once-thriving Boston industry – the manufacture of clay pipes. At one point, at least nine pipe makers earned a living in the town. This is unsurprising given that Boston was a thriving port with an almost limitless supply of tobacco and the land around the town had an abundance of good quality clay. Tobacco smoking had fallen out of favour briefly prior to the Napoleonic Wars as snuff taking became increasingly fashionable. But, by the middle third of the nineteenth century the smoking habit had built up again and several kilns were in operation, often close to the banks of the River Witham. Business was generally good for two reasons. Firstly, clay pipes were very cheap, and secondly, they had a limited lifespan, being quite brittle. Clark's, McConnell's and others all sold pipes to the public in their thousands. Remember too, Boston was a big market – a steady population of just under 40,000 in the middle of the nineteenth century, made it the second largest town in Lincolnshire. In addition, the town was an important stopover for thousands of European migrants and refugees on their way to North America.

We should remember that the dangers of smoking were largely glossed over until the 1970's – in fact up until the 1960's medical practitioners often accepted payments in return for promoting the health benefits of a regular intake of tobacco. Newspapers were once full of accounts from smokers apparently "enjoying" long life as well as smoking. Take this story from the *Boston Guardian* in 1898. The lady is from Worcestershire, but the story was read by the folk of Lincolnshire:

"Mrs Ann Smith ... attained her 110th year... the centenarian was born ... near Oxford, and has spent over a hundred years ... in a house upon wheels, while travelling about the country from fair to fair ... she generally takes four meals a day, and though she takes but sparingly of intoxicating drinks, she is an inveterate smoker, a short clay pipe being an especial friend".

Fourteen years earlier, however, the same newspaper, perhaps, subtly hinting that smokers could always give up the habit without wasting their expenditure on the pipe itself had the following advice:

"A very odd and pretty hanging basket can be made out of an old clay pipe. Fill with rich earth, and plant a few vines of creeping Charlie and Wandering Jew. Suspend from a bracket by a gold or silver braid".

For those employed in the manufacture of clay pipes, hours were long, conditions were uncomfortably hot and pay was poor. I thought of the men and boys engaged in this gruelling work when watching a recent documentary on tea drinking in India. Workers were filmed in Kolkata, digging clay from the banks of the Ganges river before moulding pieces of it into cups and then firing them in a red-hot kiln. Each "potter" made several thousand cups every day. It must have been similar for the clay pipe makers of Boston.

Finally, one industry that cannot be left out entirely but which we will just give a light touch – feathers. There was no shortage of them locally – the fens were full of geese! In 1826, Timothy Anderson opened a feather factory on Pen Street (apparently named because of several shops selling quills). Inside, tons and tons of feathers were cleaned, dried and fluffed for use in mattresses, pillows, cushions and the like. The business expanded rapidly, moving into larger premises on Bridge Street for a while before taking on an even larger factory on Trinity Street. This building was destroyed by what the *Lincolnshire Free Press* called *"the largest fire that has occurred in Boston for years"* in October 1876, resulting in Samuel Sherwin designing a new factory on the same street that opened the following year. When you visit Boston, please look for this building – close to the railway station. It still has the distinctive Swan figurehead above the date of 1877 atop the three-storey building, but unless you knew otherwise you'd never believe this elegant apartment block was once a factory.

In the final year of the nineteenth century, Edward Fogarty, at that point a minor shareholder in the business, bought the entire company and renamed it "E. Fogarty & Co.". The business has born his name ever since. The first world war naval blockades led to a temporary closure of the factory, as neither raw materials could get into Boston, or finished products leave the port safely. Fogarty himself was caught up in the early part of the war. The *Boston Guardian* carried an interview with Edward in August 1914 in which he described the scene at Ostend, as he and his wife attempted to return to England:

"When we arrived at the Quay there were tons of luggage. At about three o'clock the British Consul sent word round that all English people were advised to leave the country … As many people had travelled from Berlin, they had been standing in the train packed like sardines for about 20 hours".

Fogarty went on to describe how many of the evacuees, fearful for their lives, fled Ostend leaving luggage, even motor cars behind. When their ferry neared Dunkirk, a French naval vessel fired at them and delayed their journey for some time before being assured the boat was carrying only English passengers.

At the conclusion of the war, business resumed at a pace. We can thank the Boston Guardian once again for carrying a lengthy article in July 1919 from which we find that Fogarty was importing most of his feathers and down at the time from China, Hong Kong, Japan, Ireland and the United States. The factory had hundreds of tons of duck, chicken and goose feathers and down, being systematically snipped, cleaned and dried in order to produce the best quality mattresses, duvets and pillows for customers around the world.

Business continued to expand – by 1962, even larger premises had been purchased and the company was employing over 700 workers. By now, man-made fibres had been added to the Fogarty product range. Today, the firm is still operating from premises in Boston, and, as we have said, their large white swan continues to fly over the Lincolnshire town.

Now, after looking up, it is time to look down.

Further Reading:

H. Shinn, Boston Through Time, Amberley (2014)

R. Gurnham, The Story of Boston, History Press (2014)

U is for Underground and Underwater

You may well never have heard of the United Kingdom Warning and Monitoring Organisation. It was created by the Home Office in 1957, at a time when the prospect of an impending nuclear war was becoming increasingly likely in the eyes of many. The UKWMO had an operational lifespan of 35 years before being wound up in 1992.

Lincolnshire had 55 monitoring posts, at Alford, Bardney, Barton-on-Humber, Baumber, Billingborough, Billinghay, Binbrook, Bishop Norton, Boston, Bourne, Burgh-on-Bain, Canwick, Castle Bytham, Chapel St. Leonards, Claypole, Coningsby, Crowland, Dunham-on-Trent, East Kirkby, Eastoft, Epworth, Fosdyke, Friskney, Fulstow, Gainsborough, Grantham, Hackthorn, Heckington, Holbeach, Honington, Humberston, Ingoldsby, Little Steeping, Long Sutton, Louth, Mablethorpe, Market Deeping, Market Rasen, Moulton Chapel, Navenby, North Kelsey, North Somercotes, Old Leake, Quadring Eaudyke, Roxton, Scawby, Scotter, Skegness, Sleaford, Spalding, Sturton by Stow, Swallow, Tetford, Winterton and Wootton. Why so many, and so near to the East Coast? The perceived threat came from Russia, and the earliest warnings could be given by detecting attacks from the East. However, the primary purpose of the UKWMO was not to warn of impending bombings, but to report the effects of strikes once they had taken place.

During World War II, the role of the Royal Observer Corps was to detect and identify incoming enemy aircraft (and, subsequently, V1 and V2 missile attacks) so the Home Office made a logical choice in putting this long-standing civil defence organisation in charge of the programme.

One of the best-preserved sites is near to Holbeach. Occasionally (usually on heritage open days), the public may access the facility, but probably the easiest way to get a really good look inside is to conduct an online search, where a very good video is available to view freely from the comfort of your own home. Most people drive or walk past the site without even being aware that it exists. There is a tiny triangular field on the northern side of Washway Road (the old A17) just over a mile to the north of Holbeach. In the field, below some power cables is what looks to be little more than a concrete cube whose sides are about a metre in length. On the top is a steel access hatch. A few yards away is a much smaller concrete box – this is the ventilation shaft. Jutting out of the ground between the two is a metal pipe – this housed the all-important survey meter which could detective levels of radiation. Besides it on the ground was a "battle plate" used to measure and record the power of a bomb blast – this has now been removed.

Inside the station, the three staff, having descended via a ladder, found their workspace and accommodation to be cramped, to say the least. Power was provided by a 12volt battery pack, which could be recharged using a petrol generator. Plans suggested that personnel should expect to remain inside for up to three weeks following a nuclear attack. Bedding was only provided for two with the expectation that at least one person remained on duty at all times. The risk of flooding was a constant factor, with incumbents having to make use of a hand pump to clear out excess water. Thankfully, the station was only ever used for training programmes and the in-built warning siren never saw active service.

With the cold war apparently "thawing", the monitoring post was closed down permanently in 1991. The Holbeach facility is one of the best-preserved in the country. Others are in less good condition. For example, the monitoring post at Mablethorpe was filled in with concrete and left in the dunes to decompose over time. It can be found easily by following the path to the sea from Quebec Road, opposite the end of Links Avenue. Shortly before reaching the beach, on the right-hand side is a graffiti-covered brick box – this is all that remains.

Several other of these "bunkers" remain. Some of them reasonably accessible, others, definitely off-limits. Remember, the threat of nuclear fallout may well have receded, but you could well be risking your life visiting these relics unless you are part of an official tour. For more information on cold war defences, a chapter in my book on the Yorkshire Coast looks closely at the RAF site at Holmpton in Holderness.

Since we just mentioned Mablethorpe, let's turn our attention to a couple of species that are very much at home underground or underwater – meerkats and seals. We can find both in a single location: the Mablethorpe Seal Sanctuary and Wildlife Centre. Most people who spend time here probably do not realise that parts of the buildings began life in the second world war as a lookout point, and that prior to its present use, the site has been home to a target range and holiday accommodation. Gerald and Rene King purchased three acres of land in 1973 to establish a *"bird and animal park"*. The couple had a little experience, having operated a zoological garden in Suffolk and been a florist for some time, but as Gerald himself said, his prime motivation for change was down to being *"so fed up … we decided to do something else"*. The couple never shirked away from hard work and after 11 months intensive activity, their new venture opened its doors to the public in August 1974.

Seals didn't feature in the parks original designs but when a stranded pup was found nearby, the Kings took it in and, with some sound advice from *Natureland* at Skegness, the seal survived. More rescues followed and by the end of the 1980's a 1,000-gallon pool had been sunk and a seal hospital opened on the site. At this time, Phocine Distemper Virus was rampaging through the wild seal population and so, when a national newspaper picked up the story of what was being planned in Mablethorpe, donations of money and goods flooded in, to the extent that the original budget of £5,000 was increased by an extra £20,000.

Now, the seals have pool space almost three times as big, and the sanctuary has cared for thousands of animals over the years. In 2016, a large fire destroyed the education room and took the lives of some animals, but, with the help of voluntary donations, the sanctuary is fully operational once more.

The social behaviour of meerkats makes them a very popular attraction in any wildlife park. They tend to live in family "clans" of up to 50 meerkats. In the wild a meerkat might live for 6-7 years, but in captivity, their lifespan is often at least double. Meerkats are fierce diggers, moving their own bodyweight of sand in seconds. They dig for three reasons, firstly to make their underground burrow homes, secondly to forage for food, and thirdly, to stir up sand clouds in order to deter predators. Fortunately for visitors, although they spend a lot of time underground, there always seems to be plenty on view.

As for seals, the number to see varies according to the number being rescued at any point in time, but usually the sanctuary has anywhere between half a dozen and a dozen seals in its care. Some stay for a few hours, others much longer. In a sanctuary setting, the seals do not get to do any diving, but in the open sea, they have been recorded at depths of ½ a kilometre hunting for food, and even fighting one another over mating rights. The grey seals found more commonly locally do not dive as deep but can stay underwater for a quarter of an hour on a single breath!

Seals aren't the only species to come and go in Mablethorpe. It has a long history of being associated with communities of humans from several different lands, as we shall see.

Further Reading (and viewing!):

P. Ozorak, Underground Structures of the Cold War, Pen & Sword (2012)

Watch a short video of the story behind the Mablethorpe Seal Sanctuary at:

https://vimeo.com/102528480

V is for Vikings and other Visitors

Evidence of extended periods of Scandinavian settlement throughout the Lincolnshire coastal region can be seen by examining place names. In Norse *-thorp* or *-thorpe* meaning *hamlet*, is found in Cleethorpes, Addlethorpe, Mablethorpe, Trusthorpe, Theddlethorpe and Hogsthorpe. There is more. The suffix *-by* meaning *village* occurs at least nine times, at Grimsby, Anderby, Saltfleetby, Maltby, Beesby, Markby, Thurlby, Bilsby, and, my favourite, Sloothby.

The earliest recording I could find for Mablethorpe was the Domesday book in which it was listed as *Malbertorp*. Some say this is proof of a homestead in the ownership of a man of German descent named *Malber*, but I favour the view that it is a reference to the forest (now sunken off the coast) that included many Maple trees.

Examining the name of a town or village, therefore, can give significant clues as to the origin of the settlement. Entirely Scandinavian in origin and the settlement was most likely established by the Vikings, whereas a hybrid name, mixing Old English with, say Norse, leads observers to infer that this is an existing settlement that was taken over by the Vikings. So, for example Anderby is most likely a Viking settlement, named after a man called Anders, whereas Huttoft, derived from the Old English "Huh" and the Scandinavian suffix "-toft" would have been an existing settlement prior to the Vikings.

Either way, the facts are indisputable – immigration along the Lincolnshire coastline is not a new phenomenon. But it is a complicated set of stories. Take the movement of Jews for example. Towns like Grimsby had a significant Jewish population in Medieval times, but numbers declined steadily until a massive exodus from Eastern Europe in the second half of the nineteenth century led to as many as 5,000 Jewish migrants passing through Grimsby every year. Persecution and discrimination of Jews throughout the Russian Empire followed the assassination of Czar Alexander II in 1881. If your family were suddenly barred from buying and selling property, had your right to movement, employment and education restricted would you hesitate to emigrate if you could? Why Grimsby? It was well connected – to Europe by sea, and to the rest of England by Rail. Furthermore, prospective emigrants could purchase a single ticket to America from places like Rotterdam, Riga and Hamburg that involved travelling through Grimsby.

A few chose to stay. At the time of the 1871 census, Grimsby had a Jewish population of 87, rising to over 500 by 1911. They filled an assortment of roles in the town – watchmakers, glaziers, tailors, moneylenders, shoemakers, even a fish merchant. Records show that a synagogue was in use as long ago as 1878, with work starting on the building now known as the Sire Moses Montefiore Memorial Synagogue seven years later. In 1901, Grimsby was one of only 10 English towns and cities with an immigrant population more than 1%. At that time, there were no real restrictions on immigration. If you came and wanted to stay, you stayed – no questions asked. By 1903, though with migrant numbers increasingly steadily a Royal Commission into *"alien immigration"* identified Grimsby as *"a high thoroughfare for passengers"* Very few families have held down roots in the area, however. By the start of the twenty-first century, only a dozen or so Jewish families were still resident in Grimsby. So, in a period that has seen the population of Grimsby more than double to 80,000+, the Jewish population has initially quadrupled but then shrunk back to less than half its earliest size. A point that perhaps should not be lost on those who use current general migration trends to forecast a continued change in the same direction. This historical case shows that the opposite can happen.

In addition to the large numbers of nineteenth century Jewish migrants fleeing from what are now Lithuania, Estonia and Latvia, tens of thousands of Poles and Russians made the East-West journey calling, and sometimes stopping, at Grimsby. In those days, it was generally easier for passengers from Europe to enter England via one of the Humber ports, since most of the English Channel ports tended to carry freight rather than people.

Nowadays, while Britain remains (in the short-term) a member of the EU, it must comply with certain principles that underpin the union, one of which is the right of its citizens to move freely throughout the 28 nations. We should not forget that many thousands of people every year exercise their right to leave Lincolnshire in order to live abroad but let us consider the movement of people into one Lincolnshire town in particular – Boston.

In 2016, the BBC broadcast a series of programmes from the town, looking into how recent population changes affected the composition of the community. Amongst the findings reported were:

- Over 13% of the population were born in a different EU member state – most of them, from one of the Eastern Europe nations, and most of them having arrived in the last 12 years;
- The population of the town has been rising by 1.6% every year in the decade between the two most recent censuses;
- Although immigration is often suggested to be a factor behind higher levels of unemployment, the figures for Boston suggest otherwise – 4.4% of economically active citizens unemployed, being significantly lower than the national average;
- Boston continues to be a "low-pay town", the figures skewed by the disproportionately high number of agricultural labouring jobs. The national average hourly wage is £13.33, but in Boston it is £9.13, meaning that the average weekly take home pay for Bostonians is £100 lower than the national average.

The BBC also noted that landlords were exploiting many of the migrant workers, charging overly-high rates for bedsit accommodation, sometimes with ten or more adults sharing a small house. This took my mind back to the time of the Irish potato famine, when Boston, Grimsby and other towns received tens of thousands of starving people in desperate conditions. The *Stamford Mercury* had this to say in 1841:

"They (the Irish) are the best of workmen … the men reap and the women bind … As soon as the harvest is over, these laborious creatures return home with their earnings … by far the greater proportion goes to pay a most exorbitant rent for the landlords to expend in London, Paris, or filthily luxurious Naples".

Returning to the present it is also worth bearing in mind the age distribution of Boston's population. At a time when most people are living longer and the proportion of elderly people in communities is rising by as much as 3% every ten years, in Boston, according to figures published by the Lincolnshire Research Observatory in 2014, the proportion of pensioners is remaining steady at one in five. The same organisation forecast that this will rise to just over a quarter of Boston's population in the next twenty years, but will remain well below county and national averages.

How well do people from so many different backgrounds integrate in Boston? A government *"Policy Exchange Think-Tank"* analysed census returns in terms of what it calls *"identity integration"* and *"structural integration"*. The latter being a reflection of how well different ethnic groups mix with one another, while the former represents how those from minority groups actually feel. Of 160 large towns assessed for the survey, Boston came out last.

Will the situation change much post-BREXIT? That is anyone's guess, but remember that immigrants have been arriving in Lincolnshire for centuries, and historically, far more have arrived from Ireland or members of the British Commonwealth than Europe.

Arrivals of people along the Lincolnshire Coast is a topic fiercely debated by many, and has been for more than a century. Opinions are divided, and probably always will be. So, let us turn our attention to an arrival that was most definitely unwelcome – the *Watersnoodramp*.

Further Reading:

W. Marrat, The History of Lincolnshire, topographical, historical and descriptive, British Library (2011)

Also available to download free from:

https://books.google.co.uk/books/about/The_history_of_Lincolnshire.html?id=ShAHAAAAQAAJ

W is for Watersnoodramp (the great flood of 1953)

Most people in Lincolnshire describe the events that commenced during the night of 31st January 1953 as the *"Great Flood"* or *"North Sea Flood"*. In the Netherlands, where almost 2,000 people lost their lives they call it *Watersnoodramp*. This word reflects more accurately the scale of the event – what we refer to as a flood – the Dutch call a *"water emergency DISASTER"*.

Before we look specifically at the consequences for the Lincolnshire coast, we should assess the scale of the disaster in general. As well as 1,836 deaths throughout the Netherlands, at least 307 died in England, 28 in Belgium and 19 in Scotland. A further 350+ died at sea, including 133 when the ferry MV Princess Victoria sank east of Belfast. Almost 10% of all Dutch farmland was flooded, more than 30,000 animals drowned and 50,000 buildings were destroyed or badly damaged in the Netherlands alone.

The Lincolnshire Coast has a long and tragic association with storm tides – the *Grote Mandrenke* storm of 1362 flooding large swathes of the county as it killed over 25,000 people throughout western Europe. There was severe flooding in 1665 and 1674 before Britain's *"Great Storm"* lasting over a week in January 1703. In addition, Lincolnshire's coastal communities have endured the loss of countless loved ones at sea over many centuries. So, what happened on this occasion in 1953?

Two natural phenomena combined, causing a severe storm tide. The first was a higher than usual spring tide. The second was a major windstorm over the North Sea. Spring tides occur twice in every lunar orbit – coinciding with the new moon and the full moon, and are named, not after the season, but after a water *"spring"* which rises into life. Spring tides lead to higher tides than usual. On the night of this particular spring tide a huge storm was whipping up in the North Sea – January being the peak month for windstorms, this is not particularly rare, but for a large storm to coincide with a spring tide was.

Two other factors contributed to the scale of the disaster – firstly much of it unfolded during the hours of darkness, and secondly it happened at the weekend, when many of the emergency services operated on lower than usual staffing levels.

The storm began as a deep Atlantic depression which made its way around the northern waters off Scotland. This low pressure system forces sea levels up, and in the shallower North Sea, the effects become magnified and more likely to cause major problems. With only a narrow strait between Dover and Calais, the *"extra"* water is effectively forced sideways in the direction of the East Coast of Britain, and North-Western Europe. The Met Office describes a storm surge such as this one as *"possibly one of the most dramatic weather events for the East Coast"*.

At least forty people died as sea walls, embankments and protective natural dunes were washed away, such was the force behind the tidal surge. The Daily Mail called it "a giant wall of water". Mablethorpe and neighbouring Sutton-on-Sea were totally evacuated, many thousands were unable to return to their homes for months. As well as the destruction of residential property, thousands of acres of farmland lay under deep salt water – poisoning crops and leaving soil unworkable without extensive remedial work.

On Wednesday 4th February, the *Skegness Standard* described it as *"the worst flood disaster in Lincolnshire's history"*. If the newspaper had added the word "documented" to the claim, I doubt many would dispute it. At that time, Sir Robert Pattinson, chairman of the Lincolnshire River Board was estimating that it would take £1,000,000 to repair coastal defences. It would emerge much later that Sir Robert's initial stab at a figure was out by at least £50 million – in today's money, that is getting on for £1.5 billion. As well as the priceless loss of life, so much of Lincolnshire's coastal infrastructure was damaged or destroyed. Railway lines buckled, stations were flooded, roads and bridges were washed away. Power lines were brought down and sub-stations were taken out of commission as a result of water damage. Drinking water supplies were polluted, and sewage services blocked. Several schools were forced to close and medical services were severely stretched for months. Furthermore, what no-one knew that week was that things would continue to get worse before they could get better. The problem with tidal flooding is that it will come back for another go every 12 hours, so until sea defences can be fully restored, water will continue to flow into already devastated areas.

The same newspaper had a reporter on the scene in Mablethorpe – John Manning. He was able to describe frightening scenes as he battled through chest-deep water, before assisting with the evacuation of family members and neighbours. In his words *"for 200 yards the central promenade had completely collapsed, just like a pack of cards and portion which was once a putting green was just an open space"*. High Street was under at least two feet of water, most premises being badly flooded, with windows smashed and gas lamps torn down. Quebec Road was *"like a lake"* with water *"at waist height"*. Wading over flooded footpaths was dangerous as *"several man-holes had been blown out"*. The other problem was that, such had been the force of the tidal waters that tons of sand had been carried along with the crashing waves. Parts of Gibraltar Road were left under six feet of sand after the flood water receded.

Further south, Ingoldmells and Chapel St. Leonards fared no better. At least ten died and hundreds more were left homeless with *"sea defences torn to shreds, houses and bungalows flattened, caravans overturned and submerged sometimes hundreds of yards from where they had been stationed and in some cases washed out to sea"*. Much of Chapel St. Leonards remained under water for several days. With hundreds of acres of farmland flooded the fear was expressed that *"many more tides may flow over the flooded land before (the sea defences) can be repaired"*. The Butlin's holiday camp was evacuated as three feet of water flooded chalets and entertainment areas – remarkably, it re-opened for business in time for the Easter holiday season.

Other places were more fortunate – Skegness for example, appeared to suffer little more than superficial structural damage, with one councillor claiming his town was *"heaven blessed"*. Boston saw flood damage to property and farmland, but no loss of life. In fact, on the outside wall of Boston Stump, where flood levels have been marked for over 200 years, the 1953 flood can be seen to be somewhat less severe than others. Some Bostonians did have to suffer the indignity of two further flood periods in the space of a month the following year though.

Nowhere escaped the storm completely. Cleethorpes was flooded in part, ships in the Humber capsized or overturned – smaller fishing boats simply broke into pieces. Farmland was so badly affected that Parliament was told in March that *"only some 12,000 acres will be croppable this year, leaving over 100,000 acres which may need several years' recovery before they can be cropped"*. Later scientific analysis revealed that salt had seeped through the clay to depths in excess of 15cm in places. But perhaps the most remarkable part of the story, is how the people of Lincolnshire reacted. No sooner had the clean-up operation been completed by farmers in the far south of the county, where flooding had been less severe, than offers were being made to provide temporary livestock accommodation for farmers in worse-off places. So many clothes, blankets, food parcels, bars of soap and the like were donated by people in places like Kevesten, Scunthorpe and Lincoln that the coastal communities couldn't take them all and so sent shiploads over to support the victims in Holland and Belgium. In Grantham, for example, a disaster relief fund that was started with donations of £21 in the immediate aftermath of the storm, had raised £3,834 just one month later.

In the aftermaths of the floods, two key questions were raised. Firstly, could more be done to defend the coast from extreme tides, and secondly, what could be done to provide more effective flood warnings. Both issues were addressed. Up and down the Lincolnshire Coast, sea walls and other barriers have been strengthened, raised and enhanced with other protective measures. Additionally, the Storm Tide Warning Service was established. This now goes by the name of the United Kingdom Coastal Monitoring and Forecast Service. Three important features of the service are:

1. A warning service for shipping AND coastal communities;

2. An extensive network of automated remote measurement gauges, providing a mass of tidal flow and water level data in real-time; and, probably most importantly

3. A 24-hour service all year round.

As the planet continues to warm, most scientists predict that the North Sea will experience more "great storms" and the threat of further flooding is likely to become more severe over time.

Entertainment has long been an essential component of a seaside holiday. The Lincolnshire coast is no different to anywhere else in this respect, so for our next excursion, we will look at a couple of people who brought their world-famous shows to the county.

Further Reading:

M. Pollard, North Sea Surge: Story of the East Coast Floods of 1953, Dalton (1982)

J. Wright, Skegness in the Fifties – Volume 2, e-book

X is for "a cross" and two men who came across the great pond

William Frederick Cody was arguably the greatest showman who ever lived. Most people knew him as Buffalo Bill. But why is one of the United States most colourful figures featuring in a book about the Lincolnshire coast?

Cody came to the United Kingdom three times. Firstly in 1887, when on his show's opening night in London, more than 28,000 turned up. His second tour happened between 1891 and 1892, but it was his third and final visit between 1902 and 1904 that included shows in Lincolnshire.

The scale of his show was phenomenal. A troupe of more than 800 personnel went everywhere with Cody, as did 18 buffalo and up to 200 horses – all brought across the Atlantic to create the most authentic "wild west experience" possible. It was a costly show to stage, and so, night after night, Buffalo Bill performed – between 1902 and 1903, more than 300 shows were given, often twice in a day, with just a single cancellation.

When Cody brought his show to Boston on Thursday 24th September 1903, *"huge crowds greeted him"*. The *Boston Guardian* observed that the *"Sleaford Road had not seen so much traffic since Barnum & Bailey's Greatest Show on Earth"* five years earlier. The reporter noted how *"To a lively fanfare, and a roll of the drums, there galloped in, dashed around, and filed up between 150 and 200 riders, each mounted on a splendid steed"*. He described *"first and foremost came the picturesque Indians, and then followed in turn the wild-looking Russian Cossacks; the South American Gauchos; the wiry Mexicans; the daring Cowboys; Roosevelt's Rough Riders; United States Cavalrymen with the Stars and Stripes floating in the wind"*. Finally, in came *"the British Cavalrymen, one of whom bore triumphantly aloft the Union Jack"*.

When Buffalo Bill himself took to the stage, on horseback of course *"an attendant … threw up glass balls, which were nearly all brought down by the veteran Chief with unerring aim, while his steed went full speed* around the enclosure". Evidently, very impressed, the reporter called it "a magnificent piece of work".

In a way, the logistical operation was as impressive as the show itself. No sooner had the evening performance concluded than "the tents were struck and the show ground deserted; heavy rumbling wagons and long lines of riders, becloaked for the night air, were seen passing through the streets, and soon four trains passed out into the dark and "Buffalo Bill" had continued his great tour". The following day, two performances were given in Grantham, and the day after in Lincoln.

Even with ticket prices starting at just a shilling, for most people the Buffalo Bill experience was just something to read about in the newspapers. Cody did return to Lincolnshire in June 1904, giving two shows in Grimsby, before performing in Gainsborough. For those unable to see the real thing, no shortage of copycat performers touted their wares up and down the coast – these included such troupes as "Broncho Bill's Wild West Show" (presented by Johnny Swallow), "Texas Bill's Last Ride" (Texas Bill was actually William Shufflebottom, a former pub landlord from Sheffield), and "Robert Fossett's Circus, Hippodrome and Wild West Show" which offered "50 magnificent PERFORMING HORSES, PONIES and MULES" as well as "25 world-renowned STAR ARTISTES" for just 9 pence a seat. Nobody seemed to mind that Fossett and most of his cast were Irish, or that Texas Bill was a Yorkshireman, or that the nearest Johnny Swallow had been to the Wild West, was Wolverhampton in the West Midlands.

By the 1930's cinema audiences were lapping up the Wild West to the extent that "live" performances began to fall out of favour. Cinema tickets were cheaper, performances were given in dry, heated buildings in town centres rather than in muddy fields in the middle of nowhere. So, slowly and surely, the Wild West experience became a sideshow rather than the main attraction in circus performances.

Long before Buffalo Bill came to the Lincolnshire Coast, many of the people of Grimsby and Boston had already witnessed "The Greatest Show on Earth". Barnum & Bailey's American travelling circus spent the whole of 1898 and 1899 touring the United Kingdom before moving on to Europe, with two stops close to the Lincolnshire seaside. In fact, the

Boston performances on Wednesday 2nd August 1899 took place on the same site that William Cody would go on to use four years later. The *Lincolnshire Chronicle* noted that such was local interest in the circus that the courts suspended all dealings for the day and *"business in the town was at a standstill"*. A feature of Barnum & Bailey's circus – often imitated until prohibited by legislation – was the pre-show procession. I can recall from my own childhood watching excitedly as a line of caravans and wheeled cages holding back lions, tigers and bears, flanked by fire-eaters, clowns and jugglers, with a pair of brightly ornamented elephants at the head of the procession, filed past my house, signalling that the circus was back in town. The *Stamford Mercury* observed that *"at nine o'clock when the procession took place, the route was lined with thousands of spectators, and every window and balcony and point of vantage was occupied"*. The *Boston Guardian* dispatched a reporter to cover the procession:

"The band carriage, drawn by forty horses ... led the way. Then followed the carnivorous specimens – lions, tigers, leopards, panther, hyenas, bears, wolves, and other animals, borne on cars elaborately bedecked with bunting emblematic of the nations of the earth". These were followed by brightly-clothed performers, musicians and camels, which led the reporter to conclude *"it was certainly the grandest, greatest and most imposing spectacle which has ever been seen in Boston"*. Worthy of note was the fact that *"tiers of raised seats were erected for the workhouse children ... to view the procession without expense"*.

As for the two Boston performances themselves, the newspaper reported that 20,000 spectators had been in attendance, watching a bewildering array of skills, daring, courage and tomfoolery in the three-ringed circus. Of *"superlative merit"* was the *"equine entertainment of seventy horses"*, *"simultaneous mid-air feats by five groups of aerial performers"*, and *"some phenomenal efforts in the acrobatic line"*.

Although Ringling Brothers and Barnum & Bailey announced the closure of *"The Greatest Show on Earth"* early in 2017, after 146 years, the circus tradition continues to this day – but in a very different form. Nowadays, performances are still under a big top tent, but the concept of *"three rings"* is rarely seen any more. With strict welfare controls in place, animals rarely feature in any performances. Also, once a circus sets up on a site, it tends to stay for most, if not all, of the holiday season.

These two Americans and their spectacular shows definitely had an impact on the Lincolnshire coast. So now, let us turn our attention to three of the county's own sons and daughters whose written works have impacted on the lives of millions around the world.

Further Reading:

J. Noble, Around the Coast with Buffalo Bill, Hutton Press (1999)

C. River Editors, The Greatest Show on Earth, Createspace (2014)

Y is for Yellowbellies

What is a *yellowbelly*? It is a term used throughout Lincolnshire to identify a person born in the county. How the term came to be used is not certain, with several possibilities often being cited. My personal favourite, but also, perhaps, the most unlikely, hails from Cleethorpes. The story goes something like this. Back in the days when smuggling and piracy was rife, a particularly cruel trick involved the lighting of fires on beaches to trick unsuspecting captains into steering their ships towards what they thought was a harbour beacon, only to run aground on a beach or capsize on rocks. Apparently, one such ship had its cargo seized by the people of Cleethorpes, only to find that it contained rolls of bright yellow linen. Unable to sell such material on the open market, much of it was cut and sewn to make undergarments. The people wearing these lurid vests then became the yellow bellies.

Other suggestions include these two posted by readers of the Lincolnshire Echo in 1938. One C. W. Wakerley believed *"the many small rivers ... of our county ... abound with eels ... with yellow bellies"*, while a Mr. Illman reckoned it came from the saying *"here comes the yellow belly"* used when sighting the arrival of a stage coach as *"the body work of the coaches running through Lincolnshire was all painted yellow as a distinction"*. Another noted that in one region of France famed for its corn and ground maize, locals are known as *"ventres jaunes"* and that given the extent of corn growing in Lincolnshire, perhaps this is the reason for the nickname. Finally, J. A. Howard suggested *"it originated in the yellow waistcoat ... which was part of the (Lincolnshire) regiments first uniform"*.

Perhaps Farmer and Henley, in their seven-volume *Slang and its Analogues* gave us the best clue when they defined a yellowbelly simply as *"a Lincolnshire Fen-man"*. The *Boston Guardian* came to the same conclusion in 1940, observing *"Reclamation operations necessitated much digging of (deep) ditches ... through yellow heavy clay"* leading to the gangs of diggers becoming *"plastered all down the front with yellow mud"*. Maybe, the name had its beginnings in the seventeenth century days of Vermuyden and his contemporaries from Holland after all?

Whichever account you prefer, what cannot be disputed is that the Lincolnshire coastline has produced some very noteworthy yellowbellies, so here are a few, some you are very likely to know about, others, perhaps less well-known.

Rodney Lynn Temperton was born in Cleethorpes on 9th October 1949. He was keen on music from an early age – a drum kit being one of his proudest possessions. When he got his first job, working for Ross, processing Fish Fingers in Grimsby, I doubt he, or anyone else, thought he would go on to work on the other side of the Atlantic Ocean with the likes of Michael Jackson. Rod got his big musical break as a member of the band *Heatwave*, who had a platinum-selling global hit record in 1977, written by Temperton – *Boogie Nights*. Other members of the band were serving in the armed forces at the time, so Temperton had to move to Worms in Germany. The disco-funk style of Heatwave caught the attention of American record producer Quincy Jones, and two years later, Rod was writing songs for the new Michael Jackson album – *Off the Wall* including *"Rock With You"*. By 1982, Temperton was living in Beverly Hill, California. It was here that he wrote a song, originally titled *"Starlight"* and then *"Midnight Man"*, which would go on to become the title track for the world's biggest selling album of all time – *Thriller*. Rod also played synthesizers and was responsible for vocal and rhythm arrangements.

In a musical career spanning five decades, Rod also wrote songs for George Benson, Donna Summer, Herbie Hancock and many others. He was reputedly worth well over $100 million dollars when he died in 2016 in London following a battle with cancer.

Ten miles inland from Chapel St. Leonards is the tiny village of Somersby. In 1809, Somersby was home to a man who would go on to become Vicar of Grimsby in 1815. But that is not the reason why Somersby features here. His wife, Elizabeth, gave birth in August of 1809 to a son, who at the age of 41 would become Poet Laureate. Alfred Tennyson was a regular visitor to Mablethorpe and liked the seaside town so much that when Jackson, the Louth printer, paid him and his older brother Charles £20 for a short volume titled *"Poems by Two Brothers"*, the pair spent the money hiring a carriage to take them both to their favourite *"waste shore"*. Although Tennyson spent just a handful of years of his adult life in

Lincolnshire, he adored Mablethorpe. His memories of times spent on the seafront found their way into several of his works including this segment from "the last tournament":

"as the crest of some slow-arching wave,
Heard in dead night along that table shore,
Drops flat, and after the great waters break
Whitening for half a league, and thin themselves,
Far over sands marbled with moon and cloud,
From less and less to nothing."

Tennyson stayed in at least three different lodging-houses at Mablethorpe between 1818 and 1843. One was *"Ingoldby House"* on Quebec Road, no more than a few brisk paces over the dunes to the sea. The house is still standing but uses a different name now. A second, *"Tennyson Cottage"* can be found hidden behind other, more recent houses just off Quebec Road. Finally, in his later visits to the Lincolnshire Coat, he is known to have taken lodgings with Mrs. Wiliman at her *"Marine Villa"* home on the High Street, close to the *"pullover"*.

Some say that the poet was not that fond of Mablethorpe, citing these lines from a poem published in 1850, but probably written around 1833:

"And here again I come & only find
The drain-cut levels of the marshy lea,
Gray sandbanks & pale sunsets, dreary wind,
Dim shores, dense rains & heavy-clouded sea"

Yet, why would he keep on returning if those lines represented his entire feelings? The answer is that they did not. More than 100 years later it emerged that part of the "Mablethorpe" poem had been edited and that what came next revealed exactly how Tennyson felt:

"Yet tho perchance no tract of earth have more
Unlikeness to the fair Ionian plain
I love the place that I have loved before"

Tennyson succeeded William Wordsworth as Poet Laureate in 1850 and lived for a further 42 years – none of them in Lincolnshire. He died in Sussex at the age of 83.

Thirty-four years after the death of Lord Tennyson, Elizabeth Jennings was born in Boston, where her father, Cecil was stationed as chief medical officer for the county of Lincolnshire. She was forced to move to Oxford at the age of six when Cecil was promoted, and spent the rest of her life in the city or in London. Elizabeth became one of Britain's most popular and successful female poets – enduring many emotional and spiritual challenges along the way. Jennings was raised in the Roman Catholic religion – in Boston, remember, whose skyline is dominated by St. Botolph's Anglican church – the "Stump". Like so many natives of Boston over the centuries, she questioned her faith in her early years, before strengthening her grip on Catholicism after a trip to Rome. Elizabeth once explained that because religion was *"a real and important part of my life"* it tended to give her a lot of worries. Lincolnshire is mentioned in her writing *"a flat land of sugar beet and tulips"*. She wrote prolifically – more than 20 books and collections – but said little about her personal Lincolnshire childhood. In one poem, *"A bird in the house"*, she recalls being *"four or five"* years old and being

"taken down to the green
Asparagus beds, the cut lawn, and the smell of it
Comes each summer after rain when white returns".

Lincolnshire is known for the quality of its asparagus crop – the cropping season of six to eight weeks traditionally starts on St. Georges Day (April 23rd) every year. Asparagus is farmed on several sites around Boston.

Elizabeth Joan Jennings died in Oxfordshire in 2001 at the age of 75 and will always be remembered as a yellowbelly.

The influence these three writers of lines from Lincolnshire have had on the lives of millions cannot be measured. Neither can the effect of a single line created in 1851 that passes through the Lincolnshire Coast.

Further Reading:

E. Jennings, Collected Poems, Carcanet Press (1987)

Andrew Lang's biography of Tennyson is available online in several formats

Z is for Zero

You've probably never heard of William Airy. William was a yellowbelly, originally a farmer, living in the tiny North Lincolnshire village of Luddington, just a couple of miles south of the conflux of the Ouse and Trent rivers before they go on to fill the Humber estuary. As a young man, he educated himself, became a tax inspector, and moved with his wife Ann to Alnwick in Northumberland to take up a more senior position in the Excise department. It was here that their first son, George, was born on 27th July 1801. A year later, following another promotion, the family was on the move again, this time to Hereford. At the age of 10, George Biddell Airy was sent away to boarding school in Colchester. George was fascinated by his father's love of figures, and, from the age of 13, spent several summers with his uncle in Suffolk, where he met Thomas Clarkson, the abolitionist. Clarkson used his connections at Cambridge University to get George a place studying mathematics as a *sizar* (similar to a scholarship – students work as servants in exchange for lower university fees) at Trinity College.

In June 1835, George was appointed the seventh Astronomer Royal, succeeding John Pond. A couple of years earlier, Pond had been responsible for the installation of a *"time ball"* on the roof of the Greenwich Observatory. The *"ball"* drops at exactly 1pm every day, making it the world's first automated and regulated time signal – an invaluable tool for mariners in the Thames at the time.

At this point you might be wondering what this has all got to do with the Lincolnshire Coast? When George became Astronomer Royal, the concept of longitude was beginning to be properly understood and used by mariners and cartographers, but there was no globally agreed standard – no defined base or home – no *"meridian"*. In fact, the Greenwich Observatory had made three earlier attempts to do so, but none had gained international acceptance. In 1851, following a review of the calculations used previously, and in light of his own data, Airy declared a new position for the *"Greenwich Meridian"*. It took a further 33 years before U.S. President Chester A. Arthur convened the *"International Meridian Conference"* in Washington. The purpose? At the time, many nations were all using their own "prime meridian" to split the world into arbitrary western and eastern hemispheres. Most countries agreed that unification was in order, but squabbled over whose line to use. In 1871, an earlier conference in Antwerp had proposed to use Airy's line, but words never became deeds. The United States rail companies could not cope with timetables operating to up to 100 differing time zones – and neither could their paying passengers. Something needed to be done – hence President Arthur's 1884 conference.

Twenty-six nations were represented and the crucial vote took place on 13th October 1884. Only the Dominican Republic (at that time known as San Domingo) voted against Greenwich. The French abstained, but with 22 nations voting in favour of Greenwich, the world finally had a globally accepted position for zero degrees longitude, and, just as importantly, a way to create time zones so that trains no longer arrived in one place before they'd left another!

The *Boston Guardian* covered the vote in its *"News in a Nutshell"* section:

> *"The International Prime Meridian Conference in Washington has at length adopted a resolution in favour of Greenwich. The French did not vote"*.

By the way, the French government, unhappy to have lost out in the vote, took another 27 years before accepting Greenwich as *"the"* prime meridian.

And that was that. Zero degrees – the Greenwich Meridian as everyone knows it, passes through eight nations – England, France and Spain in Europe, and the five African countries of Algeria, Mali, Togo, Burkina Faso and Ghana. Louth is generally accepted to be the most northerly town in the world that the line passes through, although it does get very, very, close to the edge of Boston and Holbeach. And, if you are a resident of Cleethorpes, you might argue this point, especially since "Meridian Road", "Meridian Park" and "Meridian Point Craft Centre" all give away the fact that the line (which is even marked on the floor as "this is the line of the Greenwich Meridian") runs into the sea just to the east of the seaside town.

Just to bring it all up to date, it should be noted that Airy's meridian line has since been superseded by the International Reference Meridian which considers tectonic shift – the whole of Lincolnshire for example is drifting about an inch north-eastwards every year. So, as of 2017, the Greenwich Meridian markers that you can see throughout Lincolnshire are all actually out of place by up to 100 yards – but that will not matter a jot when you are standing having your photograph taken with one foot in the Western Hemisphere and the other in the East!

So, where can you go to see these markers?

The most southerly coastal markers in the county are six miles inland from the Wash in the Holbeach area. There are more markers further south including a lovely stone just outside Fleet, but I considered these to be too far from the coast to warrant closer examination.

In Holbeach, unsurprisingly, Meridian Walk is our first port of call. Here it is the name of the road itself that signals the zero-longitude line. A little further north at the junction of the Spalding Road and Wignals Gate the meridian is commemorated with a very attractive millstone erected by the East Elloe District Council in June 1959. Moving a mile onwards, the meridian cuts through the A17 and is marked (although, sadly, not very clearly) by three plastic discs bearing the words "Millennium Tree Line". The discs themselves were provided by Tri-Pack of Grimsby, while the tree planting project itself was the brainchild of Dr. Patrick Roper, with the support of Greenwich University. The dream was to plant a line of trees along as much of the meridian line as possible so that it would be visible from space. The reality was that very little existed by way of mapping the line and so much of it was on private land as to make permission for tree planting an administrative and legal nightmare. In the end, a few hundred trees were planted, most notably in the South of Lincolnshire, and the project ceased operations after a couple of years.

To the south of Boston, at Frampton Marsh beside the Frampton Road are three markers – placed at the feet of trees planted by the Tree Council in 1999. Each post reads *"This tree marks the GREENWICH MERIDIAN and celebrates the Tree Council's 25th Anniversary"*. In Boston itself stands a rather special plaque commemorating the centenary of President Arthur's 1884 conference. It should be relatively easy to find – at the side of

Meridian Road! To reach it requires a drive down Meridian Close off the main Boston – Freiston Road.

Leaving Boston behind and travelling northwards along the A16 Spilsby Road, a single tall tree stands on the western side of the road – it may well be a poplar. Almost unbelievably, this giant was a sapling when planted in February 1998 – one of the final trees lodged as part of the Millennium Tree Line. On a slightly quieter road, Hale Lane (the B1184), near Sibsey, stands a metal plaque on a metre-tall pole, placed in 2002 to mark the Queen's Golden Jubilee Year.

Possibly my favourite, is the plaque sited a little north of the tiny village of Stickney in 2005. I accept that at 8 miles from the sea, we are stretching the limits of what constitutes *"coastal"* here, but I include it for the following reason. The plaque is worded as follows:

"The Greenwich Meridian, chosen as the Prime Meridian in 1884, passes through this point. Measurement of longitude was made possible by the development of an accurate maritime chronometer by Lincolnshire-based clockmaker John Harrison of Barrow-on-Humber (1693 – 1776)".

So, there you have it – we have a yellowbelly to thank for the Prime Meridian, and another one for the measurement of longitude itself! Or do we? Harrison definitely spent more than 35 years living, and working in Lincolnshire, a mile and a half south of the Humber estuary in the village of Barrow, but he was born in Yorkshire. The story goes that he was so fascinated by the mechanisms of a watch given to him at the age of six that when he started working alongside his father in carpentry, he sought out clocks to repair and rebuild, before combining both sets of skills to manufacturer his own timepieces. Three of his very early clocks can still be seen, unfortunately not in Lincolnshire. However, at around the age of 30, Harrison received a commission to make a stable house clock for the Pelham family at Brocklesby Park in North Lincolnshire. This is still working – Brocklesby being a couple of miles south-west of Immingham.

Sometime around 1727 John decided to move to London – tempted by the 1714 Longitude Act's promise of rewards up to £20,000 for the inventor of a device capable of accurately measuring and maintaining time whilst at sea. There he met and worked with Edmund Halley before returning to Barrow to work on his first prototype. He chose Barrow for three reasons – firstly he already had a workshop there, secondly, he had a willing and capable helper – his own brother James, and thirdly, there he had ready access to the open sea via the Humber.

By May 1936, Harrison's first design was ready for a public trial at sea. Results from a voyage to Lisbon and back were so promising that the "Longitude Board" paid John a reward of £250 with a further £250 if he could improve the accuracy of his system. Shortly afterwards Harrison moved to London, this time for good.

It took a further 28 years and three more prototypes before a final test in 1764. By now John's son William, born in Barrow in 1728 and an accomplished instrument maker in his own right was working regularly on the project with his father. The test required a two-month voyage to Jamaica and with John now in his seventies, William sailed with the device.

Results were so good that the Longitude Board closed the rewards offer to any further entrants and William himself (a true yellowbelly remember!) was elected a Fellow of the Royal Society.

However, the story turns somewhat sour at this point. John's main competitor, a man by the name of Nevil Maskelyne, had just been elected Astronomer Royal, a position with a seat at Greenwich on the Longitude Board. When Harrison claimed the £20,000 reward the board raised a series of objections, leading to John having to design yet another improved timepiece and appeal directly to Parliament for his remuneration. It took the King himself to speak up on Harrison's behalf before Parliament (not the board, note) finally awarded him £8,750 in his eightieth year. He died three years later. Father and son are buried together in London.

Barrow-upon-Humber is a little way to the west of the Greenwich Meridian line when it leaves the county of Lincolnshire for good at the southern end of Cleethorpes. The metal line in the ground marking this was made from stainless steel by Hadfield's of Sheffield and donated to Cleethorpes in the 1930's. Walking along Meridian Road, there is a more obvious landmark to spot. In 2015 a stunning granite globe was unveiled besides the steel ribbon meridian line. Standing 143 miles north of London on a cuboid plinth engraved with the words *"The World revolves around Cleethorpes"* it is an impressive site. Two things stand out. Firstly, how little land the meridian line actually passes through – more than three quarters of it cuts through water. Secondly, the globe serves to illustrate very clearly just how far north of the equator Lincolnshire is – being 1,000 miles closer to the North Pole, in fact. The Arctic Circle is closer than the Tropic of Cancer to Cleethorpes – something most *"Meggies"* know only too well, especially when the wind is blowing in from the North East.

A final thought for you, perhaps as you straddle the Meridian. The stainless steel line at Cleethorpes runs diagonally across a footpath before ending in an arrow pointing out to sea where your eye will inevitably fall on shipping, navigating routes made possible by the endeavours of dedicated and skilled Lincolnshire folk. Then cast your gaze beyond the water to Spurn Point on the Yorkshire Coast where there is another story to be told in a different book.

Further Reading:

George Biddell Airy's Autobiography is widely available to read online

D. Sobel, Longitude, Harper Press (2005)

D. Leslie, The Yorkshire Coast from A to Z, e-book (2016)

Before you go

The cover photograph used in the paperback edition was taken by the author who retains copyright.

The front cover photograph of Donna Nook used in the e-book edition is the work of Angus Townley who kindly gave consent to use his Wikimedia Commons image:

[CC BY-SA 2.0 (http://creativecommons.org/licenses/by-sa/2.0)]

The brief extract attributed to Dr. Alan Dowling is from:

http://friendsofcleethorpesheritage.co.uk/home/alan-dowling-articles

Dr. Dowling retains the copyright to this. Any re-use of this extract should also acknowledge him as the original source.

David Leslie publishes exclusively via Amazon – to give low prices for the reader, and to avoid the use of paper.

The Kindle App is freely available for most platforms.

"The Yorkshire Coast From A to Z" is also available – in two formats. Readers have the option, for a slightly higher price, to include 50 online tour maps in the purchase.

David has also published "Extraordinary Times" – a meandering set of true stories, all with some family connection to the author.

Look out for more publications in the "A to Z" series:

Coming soon ... The Antrim Coast, The Yorkshire Dales, and ... Bolsover!

Follow David Leslie on Amazon at:

https://www.amazon.co.uk/David-Leslie/e/B01FUANIFS/ref=sr_ntt_srch_lnk_1?qid=1490465156&sr=8-1

Printed in Great Britain
by Amazon